PATROL

0   100   200

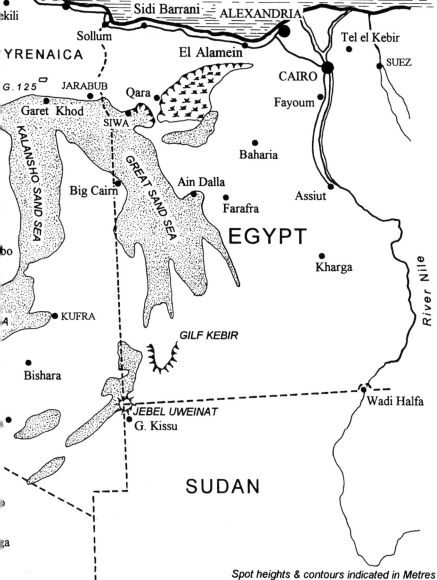

DERNA

DAR   TOBRUK   Sidi Barrani   ALEXANDRIA

ekili   Sollum   Tel el Kebir

YRENAICA   El Alamein   SUEZ

G.125   JARABUB   Qara   CAIRO

Garet Khod   Fayoum

SIWA

Baharia

Big Cairn   Ain Dalla   Assiut

bo   Farafra

EGYPT

Kharga

KUFRA

GILF KEBIR

Bishara

JEBEL UWEINAT   Wadi Halfa
G. Kissu

SUDAN

Spot heights & contours indicated in Metres

IN
ROMMEL'S
BACKYARD

"For years we lived with one another in the naked desert, under the indifferent heaven. By day the hot sun fermented us; and we were dizzied by the beating wind. At night we were stained by dew, and shamed into pettiness by the innumerable silences of stars".

Seven Pillars of Wisdom
T.E.LAWRENCE

IN
ROMMEL'S
BACKYARD

A Memoir of
The Long Range Desert Group

by
ALASTAIR TIMPSON
with
Andrew Gibson-Watt

Foreword by
Major-General David Lloyd Owen
CB, DSO, OBE, MC

LEO COOPER

First published in Great Britain in 2000 by
LEO COOPER
an imprint of
Pen & Sword Books
47 Church Street
Barnsley
South Yorkshire
S70 2AS

ISBN 085052 714 7

A catalogue record for this book
is available from the British Library

Typeset in 11/13pt Candida by
Phoenix Typesetting, Ilkley, West Yorkshire

Printed in England by
Redwood Books Ltd, Trowbridge, Wilts.

CONTENTS

FOREWORD
by
Major General David Lloyd Owen
CB, DSO, OBE, MC
Chairman, The Long Range Desert Group
Association

I sometimes wonder why it is that so many people are still intrigued by stories of war. Then, when I think about it, I come to the conclusion that the routine of life in this modern world does not offer many opportunities to those who would like to escape from dull monotony. For some it can come from reading true stories of courage and daring.

Alastair Timpson's account of his time serving with the Guards Patrol of the Long Range Desert Group is in no way exaggerated. It will almost certainly appeal to any with an imaginative streak in them.

He was in many ways a product of a rather conventional background, so he possessed an innate but extremely strong sense of duty. Yet he also had a powerful spirit of adventure in him as well as an apparently total lack of fear. These characteristics are evident throughout this very exciting narrative.

The vivid account of how he somehow managed to maintain

the Road Watch, during Rommels's retreat from Alamein in late 1942, is a masterpiece of understatement about a truly heroic achievement.

Field Marshal Alexander's Director of Military Operations at that time later told of the importance of the data being sent back by Alastair's Patrol. He described it as being "an absolutely priceless asset from an Intelligence point of view." Quite apart from that fact, it also provided a reliable source of information crucial to the verification of that obtained through ULTRA.

The citation for Alastair Timpson's Military Cross, after giving a detailed account of this Road Watch episode for which the decoration was awarded, ends thus:-

"Captain Timpson has led his Patrol on many successful and daring expeditions behind the enemy's lines during his service with the LRDG. He has always shown himself to be a leader full of great courage."

1 June 1999   David Lloyd Owen

EDITOR'S PREFACE
by
Andrew Gibson-Watt

Major J.A.L. Timpson MC, twice mentioned in despatches and twice wounded, was a Scots Guards officer in the Second World War. He died on 18 December 1997 at the age of 82, leaving a book-length typescript memoir of his experiences, initially as second-in-command and then as commander of "G" (Guards) Patrol, Long Range Desert Group during the period September 1941 – December 1942. Several appendices contained interesting assessments of personalities, and general information about the origin, organization and activities of the LRDG.

This memoir and its appendices are a fascinating record of a brave and efficient officer's activities in one of the War's most effective Special Forces organizations. For the general reader, nearly sixty years later, they are, however, in their original form, somewhat indigestible, containing as they do a mass of detail. Moreover, much of the content is rather repetitive. Although of absorbing interest to Alastair Timpson's family, to surviving Second World War veterans, and eventually (one hopes) to historians via the Imperial War Museum, the story in the opinion of the family and of former brother-officers needed to be put in more orderly form to appeal to a wider readership.

I was asked to try to do this, and this volume is the result. I have operated on the following principles:- First, this is basically one man's story of what he did. It should be explained at once that at an early stage Patrols of thirty-eight men with two officers were found to be too cumbersome: they were therefore split in two – with one officer and about eighteen men in each half-patrol – so that Alastair Timpson, although he became Commander of the whole Guards Patrol, was in fact for most of

the time only in active personal charge of one half of it –
sometimes the half described as G.1, sometimes the other half
G.2. In his memoir Alastair tried to give the half which he did
not for the time being command equal prominence with the half
which he did. The result was muddling. I have tried to make the
narrative clearer in this respect. I hope I have succeeded.

Secondly, the author's accounts of some expeditions have
been slightly condensed, to avoid repetition. Thirdly, much of
the material in the appendices to the original has been worked
into the text at appropriate places, or included in the
Introduction.

A short italicized summary of the military position at the relevant time has been inserted at the head of each chapter.

The Epilogue completes the author's personal story, dealing
with his return to his battalion and his service in it until his final
severe wound on Monte Camino which put him out of the War.
Most of this is in his own words, but Captain Ian Weston-Smith, a
brother officer in 2nd Battalion Scots Guards, has also made
a substantial contribution for which I am grateful.

The memoir is full of abbreviations which were in common use
at the time, and I have kept most of them. The reader is earnestly
advised to consult the Glossary, and to reinforce this admonition
I have placed it at the beginning of the book rather than at the
end.

The great mass of the book is in the author's own words and
is in the first person singular. My input, such as the chapter
headings and some of the Introduction, will be readily recognized: most of it, however, is based on what the author has
written.

The Introduction is in three distinct sections, the first two my
work but partly based on the author's. The first section is a
description of the area over which the conflict raged, with
a summary of the general military situation; the second is an
outline account of the operations of 22nd (later 201st) Guards
Brigade; in the third section the author takes up his tale.

Now, what of the author himself as a person? I never met him,
but of course many knew him in middle and old age, and a
number of older people must remember him from wartime days.
It is clear that he was both brave and efficient, and he seems to
have been a most enterprising person who would volunteer for
anything. His own words are, "I was a bit exploration-minded.

I loved deserts." He was also very hardy: in 1936 he walked (for a wager) the 106 miles from Trinity College, Cambridge to St. Paul's Cathedral and back again in under 24 hours – an astonishing feat. He also in that year travelled widely in French North Africa, Libya and Egypt. In the words of his obituary, "His interests were wide, his sense of humour unfailing."

Only dimly and fitfully, however, do Alastair's human personality, and the way in which he related personally to the soldiers in his Patrol, come through from this memoir. It is a meticulous record of operations carried out bravely and efficiently by highly-trained picked personnel under an officer who clearly had their full obedience and respect. But there is little more: the author seems hardly concerned to record the feelings and emotions of the men under his command – or indeed his own. There are few references to the heat of the days, the cold of the nights, or the ever-present flies. It is as if he set himself to record only what actually happened, and to exclude mention of emotions and personal relationships. Thus in some ways the memoir makes strange reading as an account of how men lived with one another for weeks on end in the desert.

But one has to remember that, whatever the author does not say, in such small units operating on their own for long periods, the formal discipline of larger military units (it is the same in the Navy) is largely superseded by mutual trust, mutual interdependence and respect and, yes, personal loyalty. Alastair must have had much more than his formal position as an officer to enable him to command so successfully; he just did not choose to write about it.

There are some clues. In an account of an early journey of Alastair's (as second-in-command to Captain Tony Hay) there is the following passage which I quote in full:-

"With our equipment there was nothing difficult about such journeys. Where Hassenein Bey and Rosita Forbes had faced the unknown twenty years before, we could confidently bivouac each night with no apprehension for the morrow. Tony Hay would say, 'We should be at Howard's Cairn by teatime tomorrow, and be nearly across the stretch of sand sea to Garet Khod by the end of the following day'. Later, 'Well, Corporal Stocker, are the stars behaving all right?' The mysterious rites of an astrofix with a theodolite are being practised in the light of a flickering torch by the navigators. 'Yes, Sir. I am just waiting

for Aldeberan to come up for a third intersection. Leach is waiting for the Greenwich time signal.' Corporal Findlay comes to
report the petrol consumption for recording in the log, and
Sergeant Penfold informs us that Scott (the fitter) has repaired
the steering on No. 6 (one of the trucks); and he has ordered
No. 4, as it is their turn, to produce the rations for the morrow.
And finally Barbour, the signaller, comes with a message from
HQ at Siwa to be decoded. After a few minutes with the key
sentences and lots of paper we discover that they only want to
know our ETA (Estimated Time of Arrival). One then readjusts
the inspection lamp fastened above one's head, leans back
on the pillow propped against the truck wheel, refills the empty
glass, and returns to reading Thomas Hardy or Tolstoy. If 'Crazy
Gang' is on the air, one must not miss that: if it is cold, the best
place is as near as possible to the blazing fire, on the windward
side.

"There were times occasionally when Corporal Stocker could
not see his stars, or Corporal Findlay's petrol showed an alarm-
ing rate of consumption and he reported we had only two spare
tyres left, or Sergeant Penfold's rations were running low, or
Barbour could not get through to Siwa, or Scott said a big end
was going on truck No. 1, and there were some appalling
occasions when nearly all these things happened at once. But
nothing much could really go wrong on a Kufra-Siwa trip – five
hundred miles, no difficult going, enemy aircraft unlikely. And
when the fire was burning low, and the rest of the Patrol asleep,
one would get into one's sleeping bag, remove the bulb from the
inspection lamp and look into the infinite silence of the night."

I think this tells us, in a roundabout way, a lot of what we
might have been told in the memoir, but have not been. We must
treat the memoir for what it is – an account of military doings,
an extraordinary record of courage, determination and endurance, written by a man who, we may be sure, was a leader
whom men would follow to the cannon's mouth.

I thank the Regimental Adjutant, Scots Guards, for allowing
me to study his records; Christopher Dowling of the Imperial
War Museum for his interest and advice; Ian Weston-Smith for
his encouragement and for his contribution to the Epilogue;
my former brother-officer Carol Mather, an early stalwart of
the SAS who took part in some of the episodes mentioned
and who has been generous with advice and recollections; and

Major-General David Lloyd Owen, a fellow LRDG Patrol Commander of Alastair's, and later the Group's Commanding Officer, who has made valuable comments, has helped with the maps, and has kindly written a Foreword.

I am indebted to Henry Wilson and Tom Hartman of the Publishers for their kind help and co-operation.

Above all, I thank Alastair's son Nicholas Timpson (himself a former Scots Guards officer whose son Lawrence is a serving officer in the Regiment today) for entrusting me with this task which I have found of absorbing interest. Too young to serve in the desert, I nevertheless, in the last six months of the campaign in Italy, encountered at many points the trail of those gallant Guardsmen who did serve there. It has been a great privilege to edit the memoirs of this brave and admirable officer.

ANDREW GIBSON-WATT

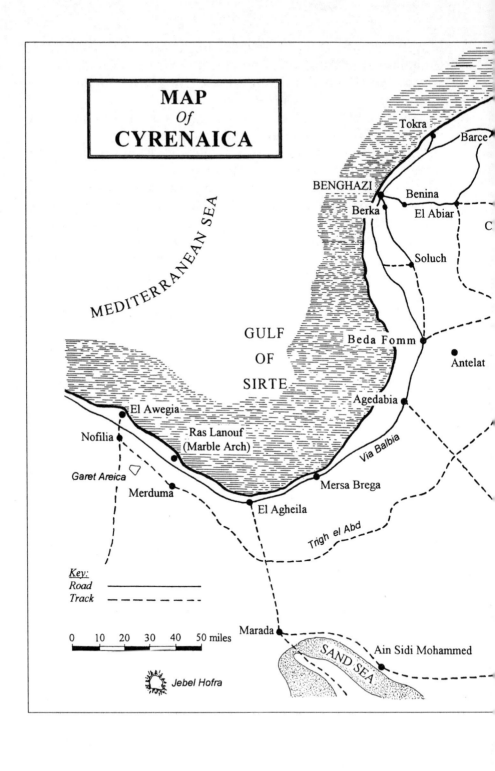

MAP
Of
CYRENAICA

MEDITERRANEAN SEA

Tokra

Barce

BENGHAZI

Benina

Berka

El Abiar

C

Soluch

GULF

OF

SIRTE

Beda Fomm

Antelat

Agedabia

El Awegia

Nofilia

Ras Lanouf
(Marble Arch)

Via Balbia

Garet Areica

Merduma

Mersa Brega

El Agheila

Trigh el Abd

Key:
Road
Track

0   10   20   30   40   50 miles

Marada

Ain Sidi Mohammed

SAND SEA

Jebel Hofra

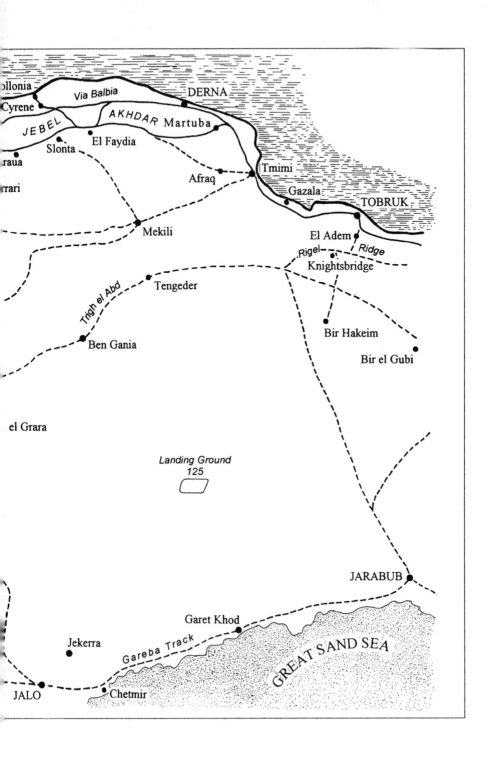

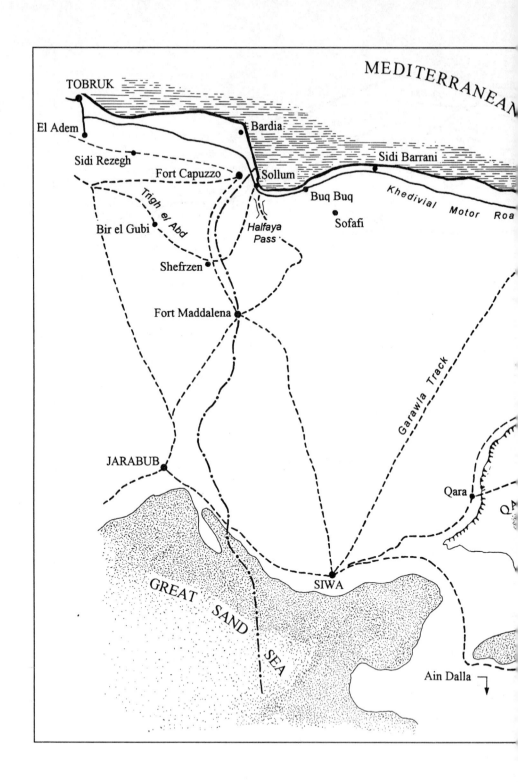

MEDITERRANEAN

TOBRUK

El Adem

Bardia

Sidi Rezegh

Fort Capuzzo
Sollum

Sidi Barrani

Trigh el Abd

Buq Buq

Khedivial Motor Road

Bir el Gubi

Halfaya
Pass

Sofafi

Shefrzen

Fort Maddalena

Garawla Track

JARABUB

Qara

QA

GREAT SAND SEA

SIWA

Ain Dalla

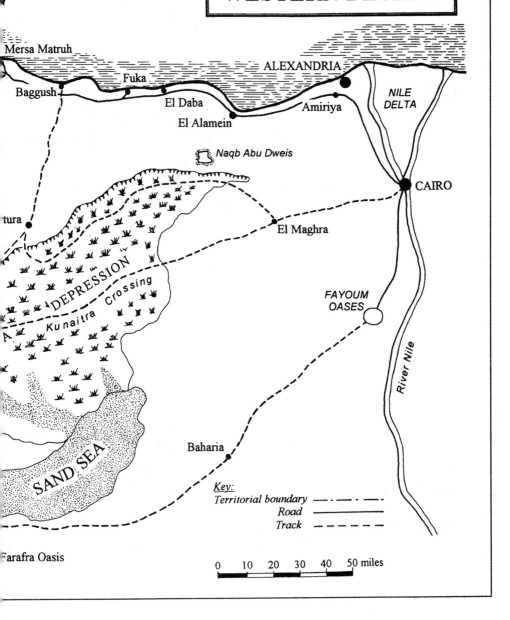

MAP
Of The
WESTERN DESERT

Mersa Matruh

ALEXANDRIA

Fuka

Baggush

El Daba

Amiriya

NILE
DELTA

El Alamein

Naqb Abu Dweis

CAIRO

tura

El Maghra

DEPRESSION

Kunaitra Crossing

FAYOUM
OASES

A

River Nile

SAND SEA

Baharia

Farafra Oasis

Key:
Territorial boundary ___.___.___
Road _____
Track _ _ _ _ _ _

0   10   20   30   40   50 miles

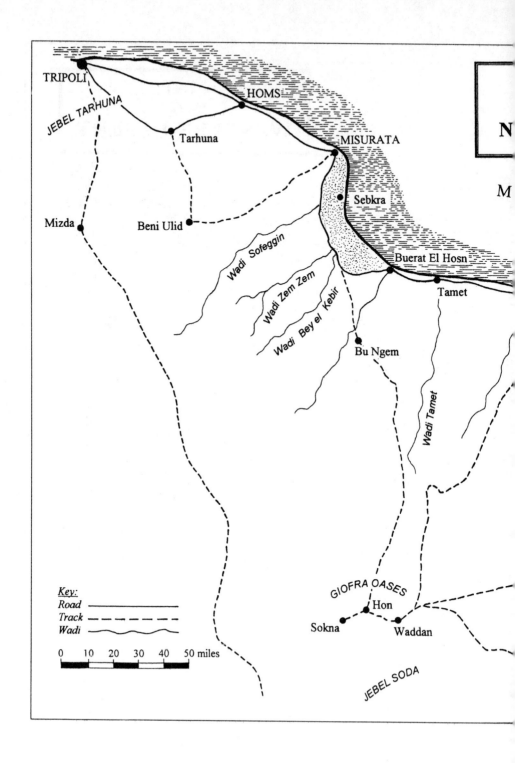

TRIPOLI

JEBEL TARHUNA

HOMS

Tarhuna

MISURATA

Mizda

Beni Ulid

Sebkra

Wadi Sofeggin

Wadi Zem Zem

Wadi Bey el Kebir

Buerat El Hosn

Tamet

Bu Ngem

Wadi Tamet

N

M

GIOFRA OASES

Hon

Sokna

Waddan

JEBEL SODA

Key:
Road ——————
Track – – – – –
Wadi ～～～～

0 10 20 30 40 50 miles

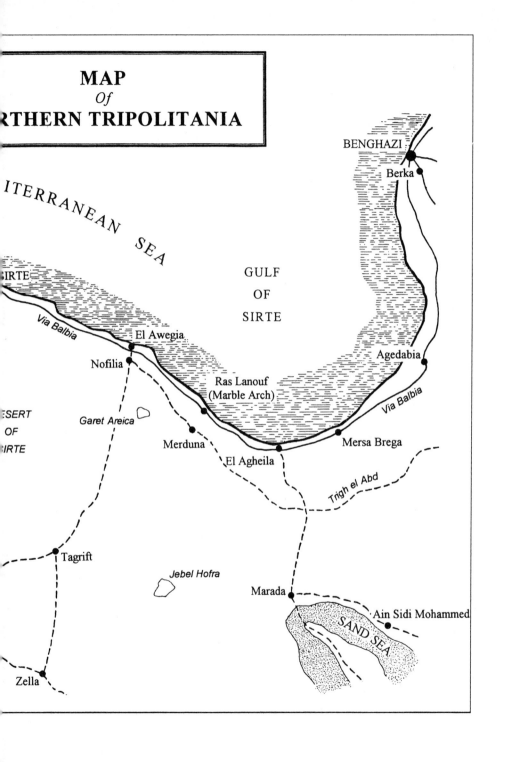

MAP
Of
RTHERN TRIPOLITANIA

BENGHAZI

Berka

ITERRANEAN SEA

IRTE

GULF

OF

SIRTE

Via Balbia

El Awegia

Nofilia

Agedabia

Ras Lanouf
(Marble Arch)

Via Balbia

ESERT

OF

IRTE

Garet Areica

Merduna

Mersa Brega

El Agheila

Trigh el Abd

Tagrift

Jebel Hofra

Marada

Ain Sidi Mohammed

SAND SEA

Zella

GLOSSARY

AA	Anti-Aircraft ("Ack Ack").
AFV	Armoured Fighting Vehicle (tank, armoured car).
BR20	Italian light bomber aircraft.
CCS	Casualty Clearing Station.
CR42	Italian biplane fighter aircraft.
D/F	Direction-Finding equipment, (hence "D/F-ed", found by such).
ETA	Estimated Time of Arrival.
Ghibli	Slow-flying Italian reconnaissance aircraft.
GHQ	General Headquarters (Middle East).
G(1)	General Staff Officer 1st Class.
GOC	General Officer Commanding.
G(R)	GHQ Branch concerned with espionage in Libya.
HQ	Headquarters.
ISLD	Inter Services Liaison Department, (another espionage organisation).
JU (87,88)	German Junkers bomber aircraft.
Keffieh	Arab headdress, often worn by LRDG.
Khamsin	Hot sand-laden southerly wind, (in Tunisia, "sirocco"; in Libya, "ghibli").
LRDG	Long Range Desert Group.
Macchi	Italian fighter aircraft.
M & V	Meat and Vegetables (tinned rations).
MDS	Medical Dressing Station.
ME (109,110)	German Messerschmitt fighter aircraft.
MO	Medical officer ("Doctor").
M/T	Motor Transport
NAAFI	Navy, Army and Air Force Institute, (the Services' tuckshop).

NCO	Non-commissioned Officer
OETA	Organization for Enemy Occupied Territory, (civil administration).
O/P	Observation Post
ORs	"Other Ranks", enlisted men.
Panzer, Pz.	German armoured forces, vehicles.
POW	Prisoner of War.
P/U	Pick-up truck, light utility vehicle.
RA	Royal Artillery.
RAF	Royal Air Force.
RAMC	Royal Army Medical Corps
RAOC	Royal Army Ordnance Corps.
RE	Royal Engineers.
REME	Corps of Royal Electrical and Mechanical Engineers.
R/V	Rendezvous, arranged meeting place.
SAS	Special Air Service.
SBS	Special Boat Service ("Seaborne SAS").
SDF	Sudan Defence Force.
Stuka	JU87, German dive-bomber aircraft.
WACO	Unarmed communications aircraft.
W/T	Wireless Telegraphy, radio.

IN
ROMMEL'S
BACKYARD

INTRODUCTION

The Editor writes:

Westwards from the green ribbon of the Nile Valley stretches for almost two thousand miles the great Sahara Desert of North Africa. Far to the west the desert meets the southern ranges of the Atlas Mountains; beyond them are the green cultivated coastal plain of Morocco and the incoming rollers of the Atlantic. We are concerned with the eastern half of this enormous, hot and arid expanse, called in Egypt in its nearer parts, "the Western Desert".

The surface of this desert varies greatly. There are stretches of flinty gravel and of rocky outcrop; there are depressions, the biggest being the Qattara Depression, a quaking bog virtually impossible for motor transport, on which the flanks of both armies were anchored at Alamein. There are also huge areas of shifting sand dunes known as "sand seas", which vehicles in skilled hands can cross with difficulty. The greatest of these sand seas lies, like a huge inverted "U", on either side of the Egyptian–Cyrenaican border, with a stretch of better going between its two arms.

There are very few people in this desert (we speak of 1940 before the oil companies started to populate it with their installations) except along the Mediterranean fringe where there are towns and villages; in the hilly Jebel Akhdar in the north of the Cyrenaican bulge the rainfall is higher and there is good grazing for animals, and therefore a sizeable nomadic population of Senussi Bedouin; they are found in smaller numbers elsewhere in the north. They were generally friendly and helpful to the British, owing to their hatred of the Italians who had oppressed them since their conquest of Libya from the Turks in 1912. In the western half of Libya, Tripolitania, the Arab population was often hostile, preferring the Germans (but not the Italians) to the British.

There are oases, which figure largely in this narrative because the LRDG used them as bases. The principal ones mentioned are Siwa in Egypt, and Jarabub and Jalo in Cyrenaica, all of which lie on the northern edge of the Great Sand Sea; and Kufra in Cyrenaica, over four hundred miles to the south. In these oases, with their thousands of date palms, the LRDG found comfortable surroundings and a settled population of peasant farmers who also proved helpful and friendly, especially when encouraged by tins of bully beef or fish.

There were maps of the desert but there was little on them and they were unreliable, especially on the Libyan side of the frontier: one of the LRDG's jobs was to improve them. In general, the desert was fairly flat, but there were hills and escarpments in the north: far away to the south-west lay the mysterious Tibesti Mountains in the French Equatorial colony of Chad, which went over to the Free French at an early stage, enabling a vital trans-Africa route for aircraft reinforcements to be established. In order to encourage these French officials and soldiers, two full LRDG Patrols, "T" (New Zealand) and "G" (Guards), made an epic long-range expedition in the winter of 1940–41, visiting Chad and Tibesti and attacking the Italian base at Murzuk in the southern Libyan province of Fezzan. Soon, the Free French under General Leclerc captured the southern Cyrenaican oasis of Kufra, which was to be an important LRDG base. Later, they made their famous march northwards, conquering the Italian bases in the Fezzan and linking up with Eighth Army as it approached Tripoli.

In 1940 a small British force in Egypt faced a hugely more powerful force of Italian and Italian-led native troops in Libya. Their commander was originally Marshal Italo Balbo, a famous aviator; he was shot down and killed by his own anti-aircraft gunners and the Italian command was then assumed by Marshal Rodolfo Graziani, who had displayed great ruthlessness in Abyssinia and also in Libya where he hanged Arabs by the hundred in "pacification" operations. He was not in fact too keen to invade Egypt but was forcefully pressed to do so by Mussolini; reluctantly, therefore, he moved his ponderous force into Egypt, and soon suffered a crushing, indeed annihilating, defeat at the hands of General O'Connor's Western Desert Force under the supreme command of General Sir Archibald Wavell, British Commander-in-Chief, Middle East Land Forces.

The British presence in Egypt was in effect a Protectorate. The Egyptian King and his Government in theory ran the country, but the actual power resided (as it had done since the days of Lord Cromer) in the British Embassy. The Egyptian Army, British trained and equipped, was small and friendly, but their country was officially neutral and they never assisted any offensive operations. If Rommel had reached Alexandria, as he nearly did, they would no doubt have been friendly to him. There was a large Italian element, which was never interned, in the cities, and consequently a total lack of security: Egypt was a spy's paradise.

The British occupying force in Egypt was small, but it operated large base and workshop installations which were to prove invaluable in the coming conflict. The troops included the nucleus of Britain's first effective armoured division, the 7th, the famous "Desert Rats". Assiduously trained by their first commander, General Hobart, a pioneer of armoured warfare, at the outbreak of hostilities they were a force to be reckoned with, as the Italians soon found out – especially as they were teamed with 4th Indian Division, a first-class regular Indian Army formation which had been brought in to reinforce Egypt.

Before the War a number of British people resident in Egypt, including soldiers, had begun to explore the nearer regions of the Western Desert, in Model T Ford cars. Their ostensible, or perhaps real, objective was to discover the lost city of Zerzura, where a Persian army had supposedly been lost in the sands. In practice, they developed expertise in desert motoring, discovering that reduced tyre pressures helped to negotiate sandy going, in navigation, which was by the celestial method employed at sea (there was almost always a good vault of stars in the Western Desert), and in wireless communication, in which Major Ralph Bagnold, an officer in the Royal Corps of Signals, was the expert leader. He also perfected the sun-compass, and subsequently became the first commander of the LRDG.

These early explorations were appreciated by General Wavell, who looked at his long unprotected south-western desert flank and thought it wise to make preparations in case the Italians tried to outflank him that way. In fact the Italians never had any such thoughts, being wedded to the comforts of the coast road, the Via Balbia, along which they were to meet their doom.

Among the British garrison in Egypt in 1939 were two Footguards battalions – 3rd Battalion Coldstream Guards in Alexandria and 2nd Battalion Scots Guards at Kasr-el-Nil Barracks in Cairo. When Italy declared war the Coldstream went into the desert as part of the Western Desert Force under General O'Connor and took part in his victorious advance. In January 1941 they came back to Egypt, to be brigaded with the Scots Guards and 1st Battalion Durham Light Infantry in 22nd Guards Brigade, commanded by Brigadier I.D. Erskine. Soon Generalleutnant Erwin Rommel arrived in Libya with German panzer forces, and drove the British back to the Egyptian frontier and into Tobruk, now to be besieged.

For the next nine months the Brigade fought in 30 Corps with 7th Armoured Division and 1st South African Division in the fluctuating warfare of that period. In January 1942 it occupied the Knightsbridge Box, around which the fiercest tank battles were to rage in the Gazala Line. The Coldstream battalion, with one company of the Scots Guards and some of their 2-pounder anti-tank guns, and supported by 2nd Regiment Royal Horse Artillery, were in the Box proper, while the main body of the Scots Guards was on the nearby Rigel Ridge. There on 12 June 1942 they were attacked by 21st Panzer Division and, despite magnificent support from their faithful South African gunners, were finally overrun at dusk by the German tanks; only a remnant managed to withdraw with the Coldstream that night.

Captain N.B. Hanmer, Royal Sussex Regiment, who visited Rigel Ridge six months later, wrote thus:

"A position which impressed me greatly was the 6-pounder anti-tank position manned by the Scots Guards. They must have fired their guns until the German tanks were right on top of them. Almost every gun had the body of a Scots Guardsman drooped across the shoulder piece or slumped over the breech. Several men were still crouching in slit trenches with rifles, as if they had continued engaging the enemy with .303 when their guns had been put out of action. There was an officer lying on his face, his finger round the trigger of a Bren gun. It made me feel rather moved to look at those guns, and see the dead men by their guns, which they seemed to serve even in death."

The 6-pounders had been delivered to the Scots Guards only as the Gazala battle was beginning, and they were not fully familiarized with them. At that period both battalions had several anti-tank platoons, instead of the usual one. The Brigade (which to avoid confusion with another formation had been renumbered first as 200th and then as 201st Guards Brigade) was now an Independent Motor Brigade and wore the black beret of armoured troops.

What was left of the Scots Guards was now withdrawn to Egypt, and the Coldstream (with 1st Bn Worcestershire Regiment and 1st Bn Sherwood Foresters also in the Brigade) moved into the fortress of Tobruk. When Rommel attacked, Brigade Headquarters was overrun and the Commanding Officer, who was there, was captured with Brigadier George Johnson. In a celebrated incident, the Coldstream refused to obey the order to surrender, and two parties under the overall command of Major H.M. Sainthill, collecting others as they went, broke out and finally seventeen Coldstream officers and 183 other ranks, with some men from other units, reached British lines. "Tim" Sainthill had remarked that surrender had not been taught in the Coldstream, and he thought it a bad time to start learning it. Some maintain that his actual first reaction to the surrender order was, "F . . . that for a game of soldiers".

A composite Guards Battalion now formed part of the Cairo defence until in September 1942 201st Guards Brigade was reformed in Syria, 6th Battalion Grenadier Guards now joining. This battalion was unfortunately to suffer very heavy casualties, as did 3rd Coldstream, at Mareth six months later. 2nd Scots Guards were in reserve at Mareth. Ten days earlier their anti-tank gunners had exacted a famous revenge on the Panzer Divisions at the defensive victory of Medenine.

201st Guards Brigade took part in the British blitzkrieg up the Medjerda Valley which finished off the Tunisian campaign; subsequently it landed at Salerno in Italy, suffering heavy casualties, and was then involved in serious fighting on Monte Camino and later on the Garigliano River. Finally, in April 1944, 201st and 24th Guards Brigades were reorganized: 6th Grenadiers and 2nd Scots Guards went home, leaving their younger men behind in other battalions in Italy. 3rd Coldstream continued in Italy in 24th Guards Brigade until February 1945 when they too went home; their younger men went to the 2nd

Battalion, which transferred from 1st to 24th Guards Brigade.

That in outline is the imperishable story of "201".

But 3rd Coldstream and 2nd Scots Guards had done one other thing – from December 1940 (the Long Range Desert Group was formed in June 1940, the very first recruits being drawn from the New Zealand Division) they had contributed volunteers to "G" (Guards) Patrol; all through the fighting in the desert the Commanding Officers of the two Battalions proved willing to allow their best men, and some of their best officers, to be seconded as volunteers to the LRDG. As the Author relates, a number of Grenadier Guardsmen also came in after their 6th Battalion joined the Brigade.

The Author now begins his own narrative:

The Long Range Desert Group in Africa provided an efficient service behind the enemy lines for the 8th Army (and its predecessor, Western Desert Force) and Middle East Headquarters. The main functions were:- Intelligence, "Taxi-Service" and "Beat-Ups". Of these functions, Intelligence was the most important.

The range was normally up to 1,200 miles, with over-loading and with some help from forward hidden petrol dumps. The expedition of "T" Patrol (New Zealand) and "G" (Guards) Patrol in the winter of 1940/41 to Murzuk in south-west Libya, to Chad and around the Tibesti was unusual. So was the journey of G.1 in January 1943 to Constantine in Algeria. The first expedition covered 4,300 miles in six weeks; the second 3,500 miles in the same time.

Apart from dropping spies to gather information indirectly, an important element in directly obtained intelligence were reports on the "going" – the terrain, whether it was good enough to enable a force of all arms to make a "left hook" around the enemy when on the offensive. Notable of these reports was that of Tony Browne's New Zealand Patrol which enabled Montgomery to outflank the enemy on 13–14 December 1942 on the El Agheila – Marada Line. Similarly, Montgomery's battle to take Tripoli in January 1943 included a left hook over the difficult Wadi Zemzem area which had been reconnoitred by the Guards Patrol I under Bernard Bruce, (assisted by Donny Player,

6

a tank expert sent for the purpose of this operation by the Northamptonshire Yeomanry). The Patrol commander acted as guide at the head of 8th Army's inland column into Tripoli on 23 January 1943.

Best known of all is "Wilder's Gap". The name was given it by Montgomery in his book *El Alamein to the River Sangro*. This was considered impassable for vehicles by the French before the war when fortifying the Libyan – Tunisian frontier, the Mareth Line, against a possible attack from the Italian colony. Nick Wilder's T.2 New Zealand Patrol found that this was not so. He found a narrow passage between the Matmata Hills on the east and the Sand Sea on the west. At considerable risk, Montgomery split his forces near Medenine, after his successful battle there. Whilst all of the infantry, and some armour, tried to crack the Mareth Line across the Wadi Zigzaou, he sent the Free French, the New Zealand Division and most of 10th Corps on a huge outflanking movement, 40 miles to the south. Western Desert Air Force did a great deal of damage to the enemy with low-flying attacks. Rommel's forces had to withdraw to their next stand at Wadi Akarit.

The most valuable intelligence function of the LRDG was known as "The Road Watch". It meant counting and describing every vehicle of the enemy on the main coastal road, the Via Balbia, and reporting every night the result by W/T (in code of course) to LRDG HQ, first at Siwa and then at Kufra, for immediate transmission to Army HQ. This type of operation was thought feasible after a successful four-day trial watch of the two main roads in the Jebel of Cyrenaica in February 1942. Three weeks later a continuous watch was established near Marble Arch, at the junction between Cyrenaica and Tripolitania. The country there was thinly populated. From early March 1942 until 13 December, except for a gap in July, August and September, no enemy vehicle or gun passed unaccounted for along the road from the main port of Tripoli to the battlegrounds of Cyrenaica to the east, day and night. The count, in fact, was for anything that passed in either direction. In November and December 1942 the increasing traffic going westwards indicated Rommel's withdrawal. The road watch had to move west from Marble Arch towards the end.

Look-outs were of two men, taking turns with the rest of the Patrol, at a distance of 200 yards from the road by day, much closer at night. The bulk of the Patrol with its vehicles would be hidden up a few miles away. A Patrol was usually on watch for 7–10 days and it took 4 days to get there from Siwa or Kufra (600 miles); so three out of the group total of ten Patrols had to be assigned to the road watch during those periods.

To help identify the tanks and guns, as well as uniforms and formation insignia, Captain Enoch Powell, then in military intelligence, used to fly down to Siwa from Cairo in a Lysander. He had an album of photographs. This could help those on the road to distinguish, from recuperators on guns or sprockets on tanks, whether an enemy convoy had got through to Tripoli, thus providing information for the Royal Navy, as well as the Army. Naval submarines and destroyers, with the help of the Air Force from Malta, were sinking well over half of Rommel's intended supplies in 1942.

"Taxi-Services" entailed taking spies or saboteurs to the Jebel of Cyrenaica or to Tripolitania; but the most demanding – and exciting – was working with David Stirling's SAS. Two LRDG Patrols picked up nearly all the survivors of "L" Detachment, the first 55 members of that famous organization, after their first drop (at night) in 8th Army's 18 November 1941 (Sidi Rezegh) battle. The two SAS parties not surprisingly missed their targets – the Gazala and Tmimi airfields – in a 40 mph gale and rain. From then on until June 1942, when they acquired transport of their own, the SAS found it far more effective to be dropped by LRDG Patrols about four miles from their targets and be picked up at the same spot about 28 hours later, after spending a day examining enemy aircraft, buildings and defences and other targets, placing their bombs and assessing the extent of the destruction. The most dangerous phase usually came next morning, when the Patrols hurried away as far as possible and camouflaged up to avoid detection and the inevitable reprisals from enemy aircraft. Jock Lewes was a victim of a ME110 in this way – a great loss to the SAS since he was the detailed planner to complement Stirling's impetuousness. Robin Gurdon of Guards Patrol 2 was killed also by a ME110 when working with the SAS near Fuka airfield (east of Mersa Matruh) in Egypt in July 1942.

"Beat-Ups" were indulged in largely to demoralize the enemy and destroy their transport, storage tanks and aircraft. But the LRDG did not go all out for destruction as did the SAS. When

Nick Wilder's Patrol destroyed about thirty-two enemy aircraft at Barce, an important garrison centre east of Benghazi, in September 1942, the LRDG did not set out to out-do the SAS which on one night in January 1942 destroyed sixty-one enemy aircraft at Tamet and Agedabia airfields. Their total score of enemy aircraft during 1942 must have been nearly 300 – a high figure since it came from a total of about 500 in the theatre at any one time.

Offensive action was sometimes demanded by Army Headquarters, particularly at times of crisis. The role of the ten Patrols at the beginning of the November 1941 battle was to watch inland roads and tracks, but this proved very dull. The enemy were using the main roads almost exclusively. Patrols were told to drive on to the main roads, particularly the coastal road. Several Patrols drove on the road at dusk with headlights blazing and fired at enemy vehicles as they came level towards them, often in large numbers. It was all a great success and a shock to the enemy.

As a rule, however, the LRDG avoided risks out of proportion to their likely success. Their personnel were well trained either as signallers, fitters, navigators or explosives experts, and in the balance of judgement that takes a long time to acquire from experience, as well as having the right instincts. Their 30-cwt trucks were of American origin specially equipped and irreplaceable. In the early days small-arms fire-power was modest, but later it included water-cooled Vickers 0.5", Breda 13.7mm, double Brownings 0.3" from the RAF and Vickers Ks – an arsenal not to risk losing. The Group was very much a team of professionals. It was formed by the explorers of the Western Desert who were in the Middle East before the War – Bagnold (a Signaller), Clayton, (Head of the Egyptian Government's Desert Surveys), Kennedy Shaw (Arabic scholar and explorer-navigator), Prendergast (Tank Corps, who owned his own aircraft), Mitford (Tank Corps and explorer). During most of the fighting after the capture of Kufra from the Italians by Leclerc's forces in the Chad in April 1941, they were commanded by Lieutenant-Colonel Guy Prendergast. He left as little as possible to chance. W/T signalling with a No 11 Set could be carried out at any distance from 150 to 1200 miles (beyond the "skipped distance"). If a Patrol missed its "call-time" twice, a neighbouring Patrol was sent to see what had gone wrong. Contingencies were planned before all operations. Security was strict. SAS Patrols used to arrive at Siwa from Kabrit, their training ground near Suez, knowing far too much about what sort of task they had ahead of them, having been informed about it in Alexandria or Cairo. LRDG Patrol commanders were not allowed to tell the members of their Patrol where they were due to operate until after they had left base – Siwa, Kufra, Fayoum or Jalo – and even they were pretty remote. The very unsuccessful effort in September 1942 to harass the enemy in a big way failed largely through lack of security. The attack on Tobruk by John Haselden and his commando from the land and a force from the Royal Navy coming from Alexandria was not properly planned. Stirling's attempt to take Benghazi was certainly over-ambitious. The Sudan Defence Force failed to take Jalo. LRDG Patrols were attached to help both the Tobruk and the Benghazi parties. The only successful operation was that at Barce under Jake Easonsmith, 2nd-in-command of the Group, with G.1 and T.2 Patrols. It succeeded because it was well planned and no one else knew about it beforehand. The switching of the target from Derna (100 miles east) to Barce only a week before the operation may also have helped preserve security.

After the early "Long Range Patrols" of the New Zealanders in the summer of 1940 there ensued five Patrols, but each split into two in October 1942, when the Group started to operate closer to the enemy lines and concealment became more difficult. Each Patrol comprised one officer, (a captain or lieutenant) and eighteen ORs excluding specialists. They rode on five 30-cwt trucks and a P/U (or, later, a jeep). This made about 200 in all Patrols until March 1942 when the Indian Long Range Squadron joined the Group. Every Patrol had one highly skilled signaller. He could usually recognize his colleagues at base by their manner of transmitting morse code. There were call-times at least once a day. A full-trained REME fitter, with an assortment of spare parts, accompanied every Patrol. Sometimes there was a medical orderly. The other members of the Patrol were non-specialist soldiers; T.1 and T.2, R.1 and R.2 were all New Zealanders (though sometimes not the officer), S.1 and S.2 were Rhodesians, G.1 and G.2 Guardsmen, half Coldstream, half Scots Guards before the last two operations in December – January 1942/43 when a few Grenadiers were brought in after the arrival of their 6th Battalion to join 201st Guards Brigade in the Middle

East. Y.1 and Y.2 Patrols, the last to be formed in the winter of 1940/41, were largely from British Yeomanry regiments.

The balance of about 300 men comprised Group HQ which acted as "B" Squadron HQ and a detached "A" Squadron, usually at Kufra. At Group HQ was the Headquarters of the important signal section, (thirty-six was their normal strength) used also by the SAS for most of its time in Libya. The Survey Section was often based in Kufra. It did mapping to replace the empty and inaccurate map sheets of the Italians. There was a section of REME fitters at both bases. The Heavy Section formed Group transport, with large Mack 10-tonners to bring supplies from Mersa Matruh to Siwa (150 miles) or from Wadi Halfa on the Nile to Kufra (600 miles). A light transport section with 3-tonners was formed in the summer of 1942 to make hidden forward dumps of petrol, ammunition, water and food, to increase the operating range and to help with emergencies.

In March 1942 an "Indian Long Range Squadron" was added. It comprised three Patrols of twelve men each and four British-born officers – thirty-six in all. They were a most useful addition, especially when the Road Watch involved three LRDG Patrols for seven months. The Indian Patrols could not undertake this sort of task, but provided invaluable support for the ten more experienced Patrols. Including the Indian Squadron, the Group was at full strength in March 1942 numbering twenty-five officers, 324 other ranks and 110 vehicles.

Patrols used 30-cwt trucks because they were the largest vehicles which could negotiate sand seas reliably. The bigger the vehicle, the greater the range; but a 3-tonner, although it can go further than the maximum for a 30-cwt – 1500 miles (carrying its own fuel) – is too clumsy for operational use, presents a large target for enemy aircraft and is not fit for crossing sand-sea dunes. The SAS, when they ceased to rely on LRDG transport to reach their targets in June 1942, were equipped with 3-tonners and Jeeps. The latter could travel 900 miles, carrying their own fuel and a second petrol tank. They were very good as fighting vehicles and handy for reconnaissance. After the summer of 1942 they were not difficult to replace. Their short range, however, made it necessary for them to have 3-tonners to provide support services fairly near at hand. The SAS had trouble with those at times when concealment and manoeu-vrability were needed. The LRDG's form of operational

11

transport for the Patrols – chiefly the 30-cwt – was the most suitable for the majority of its tasks.

There was a Medical Section under Captain Lawson, RAMC. Sometimes his orderlies went out on operations with the Patrols. He himself went out with the party of two Patrols which successfully raided Barce in September 1942. Although that was the only occasion when he accompanied Patrols on their operations in person, he was always in touch with them, as were all HQ personnel.

Navigation by sun compass, prismatic compass and astrofix with theodolite was the business of the non-specialist. Every Patrol had two well-trained navigators, usually trained by Bill Kennedy-Shaw, the Intelligence Officer.

With all their good points, however well deployed, the LRDG could not win the main battles which took place along the coast. Nor could the SAS, despite David Stirling's magnificent contribution. What happened with 30th Corps, or 13th Corps, or 10th Corps was far more important than anything the ancillary units of Western Desert Force and (later) 8th Army could achieve. At times, especially when Rommel's supply problems were more than ever acute, the SAS and LRDG must have provided some almost essential ingredient of success to the series of operations which ended after two and a half years with the occupation of Tunis and Cap Bon in May 1943. Yet, set against Montgomery's nine divisions at Alamein, the nine Italian divisions and the German Panzer Army's five divisions, the glamour which attached to irregular formations is not entirely fair. An infantryman or trooper or gunner or sapper with his unit could do little but try his best to fulfil his duty and slog it out. His likelihood of being killed or wounded was much greater.

Chapter One

IN THE BEGINNING

General Wavell's spectacular defeat of the Italian Tenth Army in the winter of 1940–41 was followed by Rommel's arrival in Libya with German Panzer forces, and his successful attack on the Western Desert Force, enfeebled by the diversion of troops to Greece. The British were forced back to the Egyptian frontier and Tobruk was left isolated under siege.

Throughout the summer of 1941 several offensive operations were mounted with the objectives of dislodging Rommel from Cyrenaica and relieving Tobruk. No success was achieved, but Rommel was also unsuccessful in his attempts to capture Tobruk.

Now, in September 1941, a larger offensive operation was under preparation. Wavell had been succeeded by General Auchinleck, with Sir Alan Cunningham in command of the newly-named 8th Army.

I was posted to the LRDG on 10 September 1941, so the casualty list reports, and indeed I was a casualty, in the 15th (Scottish) General Hospital at Cairo: not a good start, nor calculated to make a good impression on entering this hardy unit. However, luckily I got out in time not to get sacked on the start line.

To go back a little, I had been sent by my battalion, (2nd Battalion Scots Guards) then in the Sollum area facing the Germans on the Egyptian-Libyan frontier, to take over from Captain Michael Crichton Stuart as Scots Guards officer in "G" Patrol, then under the command of Captain Tony Hay (Coldstream Guards). I had, therefore, with my quarter-ton soldier servant, Thomas Wann (formerly Goalkeeper for Aberdeen Wanderers 2nd XI) and my poisoned foot, made the welcome journey to Cairo to receive instructions from Michael Crichton Stuart and my new Commanding Officer, Colonel Guy Prendergast. The latter received me in his room at Shepheard's Hotel. Though it was indeed siesta time, and the Colonel was resting on his bed, one could hardly call it by the name that denotes the period of time dividing lunch, say at the St James, and cocktails at Gezira. My Commanding Officer had actually lunched at Baggush (Western Desert Force HQ near Mersa Matruh) after breakfasting at Siwa and lunching the day before in Kufra. He had piloted his own aircraft the odd twelve hundred miles.

Guy Prendergast took over command of the LRDG just before I joined, succeeding Ralph Bagnold. Our new Commanding Officer was a pre-war explorer and was in many of Bagnold's parties. He was a member of the Royal Tank Regiment and an engineer. He owned his own aircraft with a thousand hours' experience when the war started. The LRDG bought two American-built WACO aircraft from Egyptian owners. Colonel Guy piloted and maintained one of them. Sergeant Barker, a New Zealander, flew and maintained the other. They usually flew together and they never had an accident in two years.

What I particularly admired in Guy was, first, his self-restraint in handling his command and, secondly, his painstaking precision. He felt that it was necessary to be in a position at all times to receive and give orders. That meant being next to a wireless set or telephone night and day. It also meant not leading one's men from the front, the conventional position for a brave officer. He had to deny himself "cannon's mouth" gallantry in order to be in control of a unit with normal operating ranges of five hundred miles. Flying an aircraft was his most hazardous task, and it was very dangerous. Apart from the risk of getting lost, as happened to five Blenheims stationed at Kufra and an American bomber which came down disastrously in the Great Sand Sea, the crew of which walked the wrong way, he had to fly low enough not to be seen by ME 109s and Macchis, though he could see them above him. When visiting 8th Army Headquarters he was bound to be close to enemy aircraft.

He found it galling that David Stirling should get so much praise for his daring adventures, taking a leading part in all raids, whilst he had to be at base. After operating behind the Alamein Line I once returned to Fayoum, our base near Cairo,

14

to find Guy rather bitter. "Look at all these cables I have had to deal with from your friend Stirling," was his opening remark. This incident was when David and the SAS with him had been attacking (very successfully in most people's judgement) landing grounds near Fuka and Daba. This was only a temporary lapse in the good relationship between David and Guy. The two units, SAS and LRDG, had great affinity. One cannot blame Prendergast for being a little sour about the episodes when he had to cope with what went wrong in the administration of Stirling's glamorous sorties.

Not only the SAS, but we in the LRDG, were continuously kept safe from disaster by our commanding officer's insistence on precision. Every action and its consequences had to be thought out and provided for. The foundation for such a ground-rule came with Colonel Bagnold and his wireless expertise. Prendergast continued with this strict observance of safeguards and contingencies. If a Patrol had not come up at its appointed call-time twice another unit would be sent out to investigate. As little as possible was left to chance. It resulted in extraordinarily few men or equipment getting lost, and this was vital for a unit whose skills and experience were not easily replaced.

These remarks may give the impression of a man who was apt to be cold and unapproachable. This was not so. He was companionable, as good explorers usually are. He enjoyed laughter. In a form of life which was uncertain, he was the epitome of reliability. Equipment went wrong and so did plans for their use, but Colonel Guy much reduced the fear of mistakes. I often dwell on my good fortune in having served under him.

The astounding distances over which the LRDG operated with very little fuss fascinated a newcomer, and this impression of measureless mobility was still further heightened for me at dinner that evening. Straight from the desert it was always entrancing enough to sit in Shepheard's garden with good food and wine, blue and red lights, evening dresses and tangos. And these delights were memorable above all others of their kind for the colour they gave to Colonel Guy's story, and for their contrasting background against war in distant places. It was the extreme contrast of oasis and desert that makes both, in their way, agreeable to some people at least.

Here, in Cairo, was the supreme oasis of peace and plenty,

where one stayed for a while between the long spells in the west with its dust and rock and camel-thorn, its battles of advance and battles of retreat. When out there one longed for oasis life, but if one stayed here too long one felt one did not deserve more and must be on the road again. This alternation of life gave a spur and sustenance to one's activity, of which one was conscious even at the time, and makes understandable the nostalgia of those who served in that part of Africa. It kept one going in a war which, in 1941, showed no reason to end.

So, at Shepheard's that evening, as I listened to the description by my new Commanding Officer of what the Long Range Desert Group was trying to do, I was not a little thrilled by the vista and expectations aroused. Nor should I fail to record that it was on this evening that David Stirling, whom I had known since my Cambridge days, first met Prendergast and sat at our table and told us of his operational plans for his newly formed parachute unit which he intended to use in the forthcoming offensive, which would require LRDG co-operation. We hardly dreamed at the time that we would have contributed, in the course of the next year, towards the destruction by "L" Detachment, SAS, of nearly three hundred enemy aircraft, as well as scores of vehicles, ammunition dumps, hangars and enemy personnel.

Before proceeding with my narrative of my activities in "G" Patrol, from the late summer of 1941 onwards, I make some remarks on the tactical employment of the Group as a whole and some notes on certain alterations in its composition. For it had now gained a year's experience of operations since the New Zealanders of the Long Range Patrols first traced with their wheel tracks the deserts of the south where only a few peace-time explorers had penetrated before.

The handling of unconventional units has ever been a difficult task for higher commanders, who are chiefly concerned with their main forces in the field and have little occasion to consider in detail the nature of small subsidiary units and their best tactical employment. It was quickly established that a force not comprising armour, artillery, effective anti-tank weapons and air support or, at least, good AA defence, must play a hit-and-run game and avoid prolonged engagements. Limitations in carrying out an offensive mission were liable to lead the authorities to underrate our nuisance value to the enemy whenever failure made them particularly apparent; at other times a successful raid by us or the SAS would swing to the opposite extreme. It would be presumed that it would be easy to increase the successes by sending many more motorized units into southern Libya and giving them plenty of guns, wireless sets and sun compasses. The fact that such stores and personnel were not available largely prevented the execution of some designs; nevertheless, the desert appeared over-crowded at times with units jostling one another to have a crack at the enemy's supply lines.

More enduring harm could often be done by less spectacular ventures: reconnaissance in various forms. This important fact was often not fully appreciated. Attacks by us, the SAS and other relatively small forces in the south had comparatively little strategic effect on the enemy. The destruction of the enemy's fighting strength must be the task of the main forces, and the most direct form of contribution to this end by such subsidiary forces as ours could often be best made through providing information about enemy dispositions, reinforcements, the nature and quantity of his supplies, and exact details about the country to the enemy's southern flank to assist a large-scale flanking attack by our main forces. The problems that confront an army commander can be much reduced if no lorry or tank passes between the enemy's bases and his main forces unrecorded. Such work as this provided, perhaps, the most decisive influence which the LRDG could exert on the main battles by the coast, though it was not so popular among Patrols as the bald-headed raid, and less spectacular than the daring and successful expeditions of Stirling's Special Air Service, particularly at the expense of enemy aircraft. There was no specialization in our tasks, as was the case with "L" Detachment, SAS. In fact they were of infinite variety: traffic census; conveyance of SAS and other specialized personnel and British and native spies; survey work; piloting of our main forces in the north; liaison with Leclerc's Free French in the south; as well as raids on enemy communications – whatever GHQ or 8th Army required of us in allotted order of priority. Our lack of substantial supporting weapons either in the air or on the ground made it necessary for us to operate in small numbers and to rely chiefly on surprise and concealment.

The LRDG expedition under Major Pat Clayton to the Fezzan, starting from Cairo on Boxing Day 1940 with only two Patrols, New Zealand and Guards, a total, including headquarters, of seventy-six men in twenty-four vehicles, was a feat of geography, politics and war. Its main consequences were, first, to bring the Free French into action from the only colony which had not submitted to Vichy – the Chad. Secondly it dispelled the fear that with their greatly superior numbers the Italians might interrupt, by attacking Wadi Halfa on the Nile, our communications with our forces fighting them in Abyssinia as well as in Northern Libya with Western Desert Force.

After the return of the two Patrols to Cairo in February 1941 there was much rejoicing, followed by indecision. High command had a good deal on its plate. Rommel arrived in Tripoli in February and advanced to the Egyptian frontier at Sollum. Wavell had to lose two divisions from Western Desert Force in order to implement our undertaking to help the Greeks. We lost not only Greece, but Crete as well. No wonder that effective employment of the growing LRDG took a back place in the mind of the Director of Military Operations.

In the chaotic withdrawal from the El Agheila line in the spring of 1941, when Generals O'Connor and Neame were captured, the LRDG were involved in reconnaissance and fighting actions to help our main forces near Msus and Mekili. During the summer the LRDG had no clear role – only ad hoc watch-outs far inland, which the RAF should have done more easily.

"G" (Guards) Patrol was formed around Christmas 1940 with thirty-one NCOs and Guardsmen drawn equally from 3rd Battalion Coldstream Guards and 2nd Battalion Scots Guards: there were two officers – Captain Michael Crichton Stuart, Scots Guards, in command, with Lieutenant Martin Gibbs, Coldstream Guards, as second-in-command. He was succeeded by another Coldstream Officer, Captain Tony Hay, who took command on Crichton Stuart's departure.

But an important development in organization occurred at the beginning of this period (October 1941). It was to split each Patrol into "half-Patrols", – the "half" nomenclature being dispensed with later. Instead of "G", "Y", "S", "R" and "T" Patrols, they became G.1, G.2, Y.1, Y.2, etc. This alteration was to conform with what we had learned in the course of operations, and when this change occurred it did, in fact, little more than regularize an evolution that had already taken place.

Patrol commanders had recently shown a preference for operating in smaller numbers than a full Patrol of eleven trucks and about thirty-eight men. Captain Jake Easonsmith's series of successful operations in June and July 1941 were carried out with only three to five trucks. He found, and others agreed with him, that in these small parties it was possible not only to maintain better control, but also to move about undetected, and thereby preserve the prerequisite of success, the element of surprise. The reduction in numbers was all the more necessary as we came to operate ever closer to the enemy's main lines of communication near the coast or immediately to the rear of his main forces. With, say, only four trucks one presented a small target for enemy reconnaissance pilots. It was comparatively easy to "hide up" with only a few vehicles in spite of the limited cover usually available, though there were times when a Patrol commander would have liked to see his bulky trucks dwindle to the size of a grain of sand when a pair of ME 109s was scouring round him.

When being circled by an enemy aircraft the "drill", with my Patrol at least, was to do exactly the same as I did with my truck. If on the move, we might stop, having removed or hidden any clothing of national identity, sometimes point the truck in a direction which I thought looked inoffensive, then wave in a confident and friendly manner. We gave them a cheerful salute before moving on quite slowly without looking up any more. Several times this happened in the course of my ten operations and I was never fired on when with my Patrol alone. On my first operation it was a nasty feeling when an Italian Savoia bomber with twin engines came straight at me low twice after the first circuit, but one could only go on waving and giving salutes. After it had gone I would naturally lead the Patrol at a right angle on the nearest bit of hard ground in order to lose our tracks, then hide up two to three miles away for an hour or two, well dispersed, in not too obvious cover. (Small cliff-sides were the best.) That would give them time to check our credentials by wireless.

Gradually the enemy's retaliatory action to the jabs he sustained from his southern flank became more severe and he developed better systems of reprisal. A flight of fighters would stand by ready for instant action as soon as reconnaissance aircraft reported the presence of our Patrols. Their system of checking the locations and movements of their own units appeared very vague at first, and it was not difficult for us to put doubt into the mind of a pilot contemplating attack. The enemy gradually knew better what we looked like. They were better at following our tracks and they became angry; it is hardly to be wondered at, after the destruction of eighty-five aircraft by Stirling's SAS in July 1942 near Fuka and Baggush, with some assistance from four LRDG Patrols.

And so, from the autumn of 1941 onward smaller Patrols, usually four or five trucks, became the order of the day, at least as far as the LRDG were concerned. When operating a long way from base we sometimes left a get-away truck thirty to forty miles from our target. The SAS, when they acquired their own transport and no longer relied on us for conveyance, often operated in much larger numbers. Stirling attacked Benghazi in September 1942 with eighty jeeps and nearly thirty 3-tonners, but even then he tried to travel dispersed in formations of less detectable size. And he did suffer very considerable casualties from the air, as did a party of Middle East Commandos in June 1942 attempting an attack on the Jebel country of Cyrenaica, partly on account of its unwieldy size. But both the SAS and the Commando units were essentially striking forces, and specialized in this role, and they were prepared to sacrifice immunity from detection for the better fulfillment of their enterprise. Their lack of sufficient well-trained navigators and signallers, moreover, did not permit travelling in numerous small formations. In this respect they partly had to depend on attached Patrols or personnel from the LRDG to provide means of accurate navigation and inter-communication long after they were self-contained in other ways.

For the LRDG, however, the small Patrol was better. The nature of our duties, of which less than a third comprised straightforward raids, did not demand more than twenty men. It was considered that the risk of writing off a large number of highly trained men of valuable experience was not warranted. It took three to six months to train a really good navigator. Our signallers were picked men, very difficult to replace. From October 1941 until October 1942 there were never less than eight or ten of our Patrols in the field and at vital times all were in operation. Had we depleted our numbers through avoidable casualties we might have failed GOC 8th Army or GHQ when most needed, with consequences disproportionate to the risks we had taken.

So the reader will realize that the Patrol was divided for operations into two, one of the two officers commanding each. Personnel were often inter-changed. Whether Coldstreamers or Scots Guardsmen made no difference. The senior officer (Captain) maintained control of administration so far as it was possible at intervals of meeting at base or when refitting in Cairo, but the junior officer (Lieutenant) had full responsibility for his half-Patrol on operations. Rank made no real difference. Mutual understanding was everything.

New provision for vehicle maintenance within the unit had been instituted on a very sound basis under a REME officer (Captain Ashdown). Both before and immediately after every operation Patrols had to send their trucks into unit workshops, usually at Siwa and Kufra, for overhaul and for special fittings such as gun mountings, aero compass brackets, spare tyre brackets, etc. This ensured as far as possible that our trucks were kept in good condition. Workshops at Siwa had plenty to do to straighten the chaos of our Ford 30-cwts after mountaineering on hillsides, as described later. A REME fitter was also attached to each Patrol on operations so that he could, with a fair supply of spare parts, effect repairs of some magnitude even in the field. On occasions a major spare part could be flown out to a Patrol by one of our own aircraft. Gearbox and engine changes were occasionally carried out by this means. "G" Patrol fitters performed miracles of engineering at times. Broken universal joints or track rods were concocted in some manner and in fact it became a crime on the part of any Patrol commander to abandon a truck, like a Captain in the Royal Navy losing his ship at sea.

One of the most important factors which brought about the success of the LRDG was that its founder and first commanding officer, Ralph Bagnold, was not only the leader of most of the self-funding pre-war desert exploration parties, but that he was an officer in the Royal Corps of Signals. A large signal troop was part of the core of the LRDG. It was commanded by a very able officer, Tim Heywood. At Group Headquarters, often at Siwa, as well as at the Detached

Squadron Headquarters, often at Kufra, permanent watch had to be maintained with the Patrols in the field on a variety of frequencies. There was also the rear link, or additional links, with GHQ or 8th Army HQ.

A signaller of the Royal Corps of Signals was always attached to each Patrol when on operations and was usually of exceptional ability. We invariably used W/T and simulated civilian commercial stations, sometimes a Spanish concern sending messages of a commercial nature to South America, or Turkish ones engaged in the Levant trade. At all costs Army procedure must be avoided. These precautions largely contributed to the few difficulties we apparently experienced through being D/F-ed.

It was the exception rather than the rule when one could not communicate between a Patrol and Headquarters in spite of interference which was especially bad when a battle of major importance was being waged near the coast. As Patrol Commander, and therefore a complete amateur, one would listen in and often hear two or more loud stations on one's own frequency, and yet the signaller could somehow hear, beneath all this noise, the faint piping of a message from Headquarters.

Frequencies were allotted with special reference to the distance of a Patrol's sphere of operations from base, and to the time of day, and the frequency, in turn, would determine the length of Wyndham or "end-fed" aerial. It often occurred therefore that on leaving base for an operation one could not obtain Headquarters from fifty miles to three hundred miles away, but once beyond this "skipped" distance one could intercommunicate quite easily. The greatest distance actually covered, and this was no experiment, was fifteen hundred miles in January 1941 between Cairo and French Equatorial Africa with the usual No. 11 set. All messages were in code. At first stencils were normally used, but later double transposition with key sentences, changing every day.

The LRDG possessed two aircraft of its own in spite of the RAF's initial refusal to license them. These were flown by Lieutenant-Colonel Prendergast and Sergeant Barker, later Lieutenant, New Zealand Forces, and had their special navigator. They were to enable the Commanding Officer to attend conferences at GHQ and Army HQ or to deal with problems concerning the refitting of patrols, in addition to frequent visits between Siwa and Kufra and, for a time, our bases at Jalo and Fayoum.

The aircraft were WACOs of American origin, acquired by the Egyptian Airways and bought from them by Middle East HQ. They were completely unarmed biplanes, cruising speed about 115 mph, capacity three people and a small amount of kit. When on my first flight in a WACO I was somewhat overconscious of its lack of defence and took the precaution of loading my revolver. The navigator, noticing this, turned and shouted, "Don't shoot the pilot. He's doing his best!"

But, besides the potential danger of meeting Messerschmitt 109s, the risks of travel over vast distances in all climatic conditions were great. The two aircraft normally flew together so that if one suffered engine failure the other would at least know where its companion had made a forced landing. Navigation was no easy matter. Either there were no landmarks at all, or there were too many, all of exactly similar shape. Sand sea or flat sand sheet can give no clue to navigation, however often one flies over the same area, and north of Kufra black conical hills, all alike in appearance, might well mislead a navigator who is not strong-minded enough to adhere to his calculations. It was laid down as a regulation that a pilot must always make an emergency landing and take a sun-fix with sextant if he had not reached his destination at the estimated time of arrival. Emergency landing grounds with dumps of petrol and water were made on the Kufra-Siwa and Kufra-Cairo routes.

On occasions the RAF Squadron stationed at Kufra suffered disasters in desert flying. There was one incident when five out of six Blenheims came down at different places in the desert through losing their way, all as a result of looking for one lost aircraft. Many of the crews did not survive. Our two WACOs, however, were fortunate and never met with any serious incident. Flying low and slow, they were on occasion able to look up and see enemy aircraft flying overhead.

A detachment of three 30-cwt. trucks under an officer (Captain Lazarus) carried out detailed survey work, mostly in the very unmapped areas to the north and west of Kufra where the sand seas, in particular, were of unknown extent. This was in addition to the routine topographical work done by Patrols on operations. All Patrols had to report, whatever their main task might be, on the features and the nature of the going covered by their route, and it was mainly as a result of the information gained by the network of their journeys that accurate maps were eventually made of the interior of the Libyan Desert.

Captain Enoch Powell used to keep on the wall of his office in Cairo a "Going Map". He would welcome us to call there when we could. We were invited to criticize his choice of colours to denote the state of the ground surface. Yellow was the best going, hard and smooth, like sand sheet. Dark brown was quite good, gravel, undulating with small wadi-beds and some camel-thorn; occasional dried-up mud pans were excellent, but did not last long. The purple areas were the worst, very rocky like west of Mekili. It did not include big escarpments or chaotic dune formations, since it was not a proper map of topographical features. Enoch Powell would take out a long piece of chalk and change the colour from light to dark brown on one's recommendation.

As a general rule no Patrol ever assumed that the features marked on the original Italian maps were accurate. If one came to a deep wadi or an escarpment marked on the map, but found by navigation not to coincide with one's own calculated position, the map's information was rejected. Even large parts of the coastal belt were found by experience to be three miles inaccurate in longitude. One had to allow for this when hitting the main coast road to do damage there – or just to set up a watch.

A really good navigator, in our case a guardsman trained for the purpose, was seldom more than three miles out in his dead reckoning at the end of a 200 mile day's run. When travelling by day he would calculate our position at all times by sun compass and speedometer readings. He would also have to allow for wheel slippage. On soft going this could amount to as much as ten per cent of speedometer readings.

I would tell Corporal Leach I was going on a bearing of 255° until our next stop. He would watch the shadow of the needle on the sun compass noting my *actual* course and distance on a pad of paper. I would keep as near to it as possible, but often had to alter direction to cope with obstacles or to make for an inviting pale red stretch of dry mud pan for the sake of speed. If I did this too often Leach would remonstrate at our next consultation. At night, when halted, the position calculated by dead reckoning would be checked by astrofix with theodolite, and sometimes by day through taking bearings on the sun. In order to obviate the difficulty of identifying the centre of the sun, one took the mean of the bearings of the circumference as the image of the sun crossed the vision of the theodolite from left to right. In cloudy weather during the winter these methods failed, nor could one of course use the sun compass. At night on the move one had to use the prismatic compass. No insulation from magnetic distortion was possible, so one had to get out of one's truck and stand about twenty-five yards away to get bearings. A bright star was a guide for about half an hour, shifting from left to right of it by a small margin. Allowance had to be made, of course, for the variation between magnetic and true north. But seldom more than one or two days passed without the opportunity of obtaining a correct position by sun, stars or even planets, provided that the valuable wireless truck did not become a casualty, for it contained the civilian receiving set for obtaining the Greenwich time signal, and usually the theodolite and two chronometers as well.

Such was the organization which I joined in Cairo on 10 September 1941. Now we must go out into the desert.

Chapter Two

HARD-WON SUCCESS IN CYRENAICA

8th Army's big new offensive (Operation "Crusader") started on 18 November 1941, narrowly beating Rommel, who had been planning his own attack, to the punch. Two months of heavy and often confused fighting, which included the big tank conflict at Sidi Rezegh, followed. Tobruk was relieved and its garrison joined in. Finally Rommel, worsted more by his difficulties of supply than by 8th Army, fell back across Cyrenaica. Efforts to cut him off failed, and he successfully withdrew his army into Tripolitania.

The LRDG, which had been reorganizing in the Delta, moved first to the southern oasis of Kufra and then went north to Siwa, its base for the coming operations.

Both "G" Patrols were re-equipping in Cairo from the end of August to 10 October 1941, when they left for another six months' operations, starting first at Kufra, but soon moving to Siwa to assist in the second advance westward of the Middle East forces. The period of marking time – more officially called, or miscalled, "harassing and delaying the enemy" – was soon to make way for a more active and ambitious offensive than that undertaken on the abortive 15 June, and was to take the new 8th Army for a short while to the high water-mark of General Wavell's campaign the previous winter, to the edge of Tripolitania; and this time in face of the Afrika Korps.

In this phase G.1 and G.2 Patrols carried out between them eight operations and their story is now told. It provides a fair example of all the Group's activities in this period. But it should be borne in mind that all the other Patrols were functioning in much the same way, and, although little mention can here be made of their work, about four-fifths of the operations were carried out by our companions in the other Patrols, not to mention the achievements of the Heavy Section, our own supply column, and of other departments in our Headquarters. If we, therefore, completed about eight operations, the other Patrols accounted for about thirty-two. Our pride and our disappointment did not reflect our own Patrol's doings only, but the Group's activities as a whole, as well as those in which we assisted, such as the exploits of the SAS. T.2 Patrol's raid on the aerodrome at Barce in September 1942 made each man feel he had pulled off a fine stroke. When Guardsman Matthews (G.1 Patrol), Robin Gurdon (G.2 Patrol) and Jock Lewes (SAS) were killed, the bell tolled for everyone.

The business of re-fitting in Cairo dragged on interminably. It was expected that the Patrols so engaged would be ready to leave for Kufra by the middle of September. Besides "G" Patrol, two other whole Patrols, "S" (Rhodesian) and "Y" (Yeomanry), were quartered at Abbassia barracks, and certain sections of Group headquarters as well. Their trucks cluttered up the main square and crowded the alleyways by the storerooms, but not like an orderly vehicle park, for few were stationary for long. Sometimes they were coming with more stores to fill each Patrol's establishment, and overfill it, if ways could be found, or else they were being driven back to a workshop that had just hoped to have seen the last of them, to remedy yet another mechanical defect. Then certain trucks needed adaptation to carry wireless sets and for the contrivance which enabled them to recharge wireless batteries by their own locomotion. Other workshops had not finished the gun mountings. Ordnance stores were still expecting a new consignment of vehicle spare parts, which might be lying at the bottom of the Atlantic as later happened with a consignment of Chevrolet 30-cwts. Or the chronometers and theodolites had not been returned from over-haul by the experts of precision instruments. The more work that was done, the more there still seemed to do. The garrison authorities must have longed for our migration from this confined aviary to the expanses of the west, which had been known to swallow without vestige the whole army of an ancient king, Cambyses, King of Persia, who sent an army of 40,000 to try to reach Siwa, starting from Thebes/Luxor on the Nile, a distance of about five hundred miles (Luxor is about three hundred miles south of Cairo). It was never seen again.

Yet they never showed the least animosity towards our visitation. On the contrary, the Pay Officer was always cheerfully ready with more cash at 10 am every morning to make up for the inroads into our finances which every further evening in the metropolis demanded. We would surely be gone in a few days, he argued, and so did we. Parties in Cairo and Alexandria were easily made and easily enjoyed. I was told by those who lived more permanently there that they soon grew tired of repeated festivity, yet we seldom willingly let an idle hour go by. Saturation point was never reached because indulgence sought to spread itself over future scarcity. Our garners must be filled to provide against the seven lean years, or months, ahead, as had been done in Egypt before. The wild oats that the desert boys scattered counterbalanced the multitude of sand and dust to come.

After farewell celebrations had been held, and held again, the Patrols went at last. Whether it was a large or a small item which completed their equipment and determined their departure, I do not know. Perhaps it was a mere split-pin vital to a Vickers gun, delivered post-haste on the afternoon of D-Day minus one. Some thought the cause was concerned with the senior officer's bank account. Be that as it may, on the morning of 10 October the thirty odd trucks crossed Kasr-el-Nil Bridge heading westward, passed the pyramids of Giza and set off on the nine-hundred-mile trip first south and then west for Kufra.

The oasis was a stronghold of the Sudan Defence Force, who occupied the fort on the northern escarpment and were responsible for the whole locality's defence. When we arrived, however, their position was not unassailable, for they were having a spell of mutiny. Had an enemy force arrived on the scene, such internal troubles would no doubt have been packed up and the Sudanese soldiers would have seen off the intruders. Boredom, and lack of visible hostilities and women, were the cause of the unrest. The men had not seen their wives and families for over four months. It is a custom among their tribes that if a man is absent from his wife for four months his rights of matrimony lapse, an eventuality which the personnel of the Kufra garrison had been promised would not occur. Such a

28

period of separation seemed to us relatively short. No one was rash enough in 1941 to promise any such thing. Still, one could see their point of view. Why should they not have their equivalent of the flesh-pots of Cairo which we had just left? The mutiny lapsed without broken hearts or heads.

In Kufra, at the low level of Patrol commanders, we were seldom in the know about the details of forthcoming events. We shot wild duck on one of the lakes. Sometimes we did some training. At this stage, however, it was common knowledge that something was simmering up north and we were not surprised to receive orders to go up at once to Siwa where nearly the whole LRDG was now being concentrated.

We duly reached Siwa without incident, the only slight obstacle being the eighty-mile stretch of sand sea on approaching Jarabub by what was known as the Garet Khod route. Yet even this is not difficult, the line of dunes running more or less in the same direction as our route, so that for much of the time the sensation of travelling in the trough between banked-up waves on either side resembled what the Israelites must have felt when crossing the Red Sea.

And after that it was forty miles eastward down into Jarabub in the first deep depression between huge limestone cliffs which continue in series to the east, by the lake of Melfa, past Siwa one hundred miles on, then narrowing at Qara, where they finally open out into the salt mud-flats of the Qattara Depression. Siwa, with its numerous lakes, palm trees, two villages, the ruins of the temple of Zeus Ammon, a vestige of Alexander the Great, was where we stopped and made our home.

On 13 November all Patrol commanders were summoned to receive their orders. In five days' time 8th Army (its brand-new name) under General Cunningham was to launch its long-expected offensive on the Sollum line, the Egyptian–Libyan frontier. The LRDG's main job was to report on the enemy's reaction, his troop movements and the nature of his supplies. Patrols were to take up positions at key points covering the inland routes of Cyrenaica, from the area of Bir Hakeim close to his main forces to Mekili and Agedabia further behind them. We had to be in position by the evening before D-Day and to report three times daily by W/T until further orders. That was the job of most Patrols, but a few had different orders, including picking up "L" Detachment, SAS, after their parachute attack on two aerodromes on the night of the 17ᵗʰ/18ᵗʰ. At the time our tasks seemed somewhat daring, but in relation to later operations they were tame enough. We did not include any part of the main north road, the Via Balbia, in our sphere of observation. Later, however, caution was thrown to the winds and enemy supply columns on the main north road experienced for the first time a co-ordinated raid by troops operating in the south.

Reference should here be made to two far-detached elements of the main forces which directly affected us. From Jarabub, on the frontier one hundred and fifty miles inland and at the northern edge of the Great Sand Sea ninety miles west of Siwa, Brigadier Reid's "E" Force (of roughly Brigade strength) was to attack and take the oasis of Jalo across two hundred and thirty miles of desert, and thence try to cut off the enemy at Agedabia south of Benghazi. By various ruses, including the planting of a fake map at Jalo by an LRDG Patrol, this force was to give the impression of being very formidable, at least a division strong, in the hope of drawing off the enemy's reserves from the north. In spite of insuperable problems, particularly leaking petrol tins, and a composition of too many armoured cars and not enough infantry, "E" Force took Jalo, though it had not sufficient petrol to return home had it failed, and eventually reached the coast near Agedabia. Nor did it have effective air support. And this factor brings us to the second far-flung part of our forces.

"Landing Ground 125" was established under circumstances of optimistic secrecy in the interior of Cyrenaica a hundred miles west of the frontier. With three squadrons, partly Hurricanes and partly Blenheims, under Wing Commander Whiteley, it was intended to prove a thorn in the side of the enemy and also a source of air support for "E" Force. All-too-effective counter-action by the enemy at the outset of the offensive paralysed these intentions. It was no secret to them. Yet from LRDG Patrols' point of view it was an outpost of friends, where the inmates' hospitality accorded all they had of beer and petrol. It was also the scene where I made some bad mistakes on my first operation, as explained later.

So the morning of the great day, the 18ᵗʰ, broke with LRDG eyes scrutinizing diverse tracks and the eternally anxious sky. G.1 under Captain Hay was at Bir Ben Gania on Trigh el Abd, the old slave (Abd) route of the interior, and about seventy miles SW of Mekili and 170 miles west of the Egyptian frontier. G.2, under my command, was seventy miles further south-west, in the vicinity of Agedabia at Maaten el Grara. We will follow G.1 with Tony Hay for the next fifteen days and return to G.2 and my Patrol later.

"The country was very flat," Captain Hay records in his report, "but a good place was chosen half a mile west from Trigh el Abd in which to lie up. There were no fresh vehicle marks in the vicinity. The area was full of thermos bombs which Italian aircraft were in the habit of dropping indiscriminately all over the inland tracks. Until 24 November, when we received fresh orders, no enemy vehicles were seen, only numerous aircraft, mostly Junkers 88 or Messerschmitts 110, flying backwards and forwards, in addition to a few Italian Ghibli reconnaissance aircraft scouring the country. The Patrol left Bir Ben Gania after six days on watch with orders to join G.2 Patrol for a different kind of operation."

Fresh orders issued to Patrols on 24 November were the result of the precarious situation in the great battle being fought between Sollum and Sidi Rezegh. The mere watching of enemy movements was no longer required, but instead their interruption. Communications were to be jeopardized as energetically as possible and for this purpose the main north road, the Via Balbia, was the objective, divided up into sections, and each allotted to a Patrol. Both "G" Patrols were to beat up a part of the main coastal road between Benghazi and Agedabia. G.2 Patrol unfortunately was not able to comply, as will be told later.

So, after waiting for a while, G.1 set forth for the escarpment overlooking the main road in the area of Beda Fomm, south of Benghazi, where Western Desert Force had its resounding victory over the Italian army nearly a year earlier. On the way there, however, the Patrol had an incident. They found "a large lake across their path", in the words of Captain Hay. "The Patrol then turned North in order to circumvent the lake, which first became a bog then a narrow wadi, forcing the Patrol to pass within four miles of Msus with its enemy garrison. The trucks frequently stuck in the mud, and one truck was still stuck when a Ghibli aircraft was seen searching the area. It soon discovered the Patrol and started to circle round it. The trucks finally moved on, whereat the Ghibli opened fire and dropped a few small bombs. The fire was instantly returned and in a few minutes the

Ghibli appeared to be hit and flew off, dropping a large bomb a mile away as it did so."

It was only a few minutes before the inevitable sequel. "You just leave it to us," was the probable comment of a German pilot and his gunner at Msus, on hearing the Italian's report. They loaded up with bombs and ammunition belts and duly set forth in their Junkers 87 (Stuka) to deal with the intrusive Englishmen only five miles away. They attacked each truck in turn, dropping a bomb and firing both front and rear guns. The Patrol was on the move at the time of the encounter and each truck made a right-angle turn at speed when attacked. Many bombs of different sizes were dropped, one of which failed to explode. With amazing luck no man or vehicle was hit. After exhausting its ammunition the aircraft flew off and the Patrol escaped into the dusk. G.1 Patrol remained in the area of the escarpment near the main road until 28 November, when an attack was made on the road, timed to coincide with attacks by other Patrols at different places on the road.

Tony Hay continues: "The Patrol moved to a small hill east of the road. A convoy of tankers with trailers was proceeding south and a few vehicles north. There were large gaps between vehicles. Seeking a better target, I then noticed a park of about thirty mechanized transport four miles south, just off the road behind a white building. Through binoculars many men could be seen walking about. Vehicles appeared to be stopping at this point when passing down the road. Waiting until the sun had set, our trucks moved off in single file at 50-yard intervals along a track which joined the road half a mile north of the building. We then turned south along the road. Before reaching the white building eight vehicles going north were passed. One of these vehicles had a 20mm AA gun mounted in the back with a crew of four Germans sitting round it, bolt upright and wearing steel helmets. On reaching the white building we turned off the road and passed down the line of vehicles drawn up there, throwing grenades among them and the people standing about, while our gunners blazed away with their machine guns using armour-piercing and incendiary ammunition. It is impossible to say what damage was done as the light had failed considerably by then. It had taken some time to drive down the road as 20 mph was not exceeded, this appearing to be the accepted speed for enemy traffic. The Patrol drove off without the enemy taking counter-measures and hid up some miles away in the former hiding place, where orders were received to make another attack on the next day. We did not leave the wadi until 1530 hours on the following day as air reconnaissance had been very thorough all that morning and afternoon."

Sallying forth fairly late in the day became accepted practice. If one were discovered by aircraft one did not have to withstand prolonged attack before night came on, whereas if one were caught in the morning one would be at the mercy of repeated attacks throughout the long daylight hours (as happened when Mark Pilkington was killed a year later).

"For the second attack," Hay continues, "the road was attacked further south than on the previous evening. The machine guns were taken off the trucks and lined up on top of the hill. A convoy of tankers was again seen going south (tankers were a high-priority target). When one particularly large one passed, the order to fire was given. The tanker left the road, nearly overturning while doing so, and came to rest in a few yards. The crew of two jumped out; one was instantly killed and the other was killed when he ran on to the road. 250 rounds were put into the tanker. The effect of our fire was that all oncoming traffic, both north and south of us, turned round and went in the opposite direction. That evening we received orders to return to Bir Ben Gania, whence we were later recalled to Siwa, arriving there at midday on 3 December."

Captain Hay's report ends with various topographical information such as was always provided by Patrols on returning from all kinds of operations. It will be noticed too that the habit of carefully observing enemy formations, equipment and movements asserts itself even in the midst of taking offensive action.

The sequel to G.1's raid on this occasion was discovered through wireless intercepts and captured documents later. It appears that the commander of the Agedabia garrison was under the impression that a force of very considerable size with numerous armoured cars was attacking his area, probably part of the force which the enemy knew to be advancing westward from Jarabub (Brigadier Reid's "E" Force). He sent frantic messages to the main forces in the field for reinforcements, and the movement of all traffic between Agedabia and Benghazi was practically suspended for two days.

Meanwhile other LRDG Patrols carried out similar raids on other parts of the main coastal road. The effect of these was also exaggerated. Large forces of all arms were supposed to be operating south of Agedabia, in the Jebel near Slonta, and near Tmimi.

Probably not more than seventy enemy vehicles were destroyed or seriously damaged in these raids. Success lay primarily in their moral effect on the enemy, achieved by complete surprise. Except for the LRDG/Free French attack on two Italian forts deep in the Fezzan at the beginning of the year they were the first raids made by land on the enemy's main communications far behind the front line, and hence their demoralizing effect. But as soon as the first shock wore off and the enemy realized that the forces engaged were relatively small and not part of our main fighting strength, his broken nerve was restored, so that repetitions of these tactics were never again to cause such consternation as was wrought by these first unexpected blows. But at least some results of this attack remained permanent, fostered by occasional raids by the LRDG and increasing ones by the SAS. They drew off from the enemy's main forces armoured cars and tanks to protect his convoys and aircraft for reconnaissance and retaliation, and, secondly, they produced an unwillingness to travel at dusk and by night; for there was planted in the enemy's mind the continuous fear of what might strike him from the south. This was a frustrating factor for one of my later operations when we tried to plant time-bombs surreptitiously in enemy traffic at night.

Raiding was in many ways a somewhat murderous game. Some of the transport drivers were found to be civilians. One could not delay long enough on the scene of the assault to attend to enemy wounded, and thereby add an element of mercy to one's destructive mission. Haw Haw, in his "Germany Calling", swore all kinds of reprisals on the "Dick Turpins of the Desert". Yet the highwaymen, no less than their victims, resented in general a war of Germany's choosing.

And now back to G.2 under my command on 18 November 1941 at Maaten el Grara.

We found nothing stirring on the ground, just lots of old tracks, with the wind blowing the dust and making them look still older, scattered derelict vehicles and the tar barrels which marked their bygone journeys. Yet excitement was in the air, more than metaphorically speaking.

On the second day, when on our way to investigate the main route to Jalo and gain some topographical information required by Headquarters, a two-engined Savoia took a lively interest in us. We did not see him until he was circling above us. The only thing was to drive on and behave as best we could like cheerful young Fascists: the correct form of salute, hand-waving, the gestures and expressions of friendship, laugh, clown, laugh! though one little felt like it. My guardsman co-driver exclaimed, "The other truck has stopped, Sir" (we were only two at the time). "Well, we've had it!" I said. (Other trucks in my Patrol were supposed to do the same as I did.) But the real Fascists were luckily naïve enough and, after a few shallow dives in which they measured us in their sights without pulling the trigger, they flew off. And we, after a right-angle turn on hard ground to lose our tracks, made for the cover of a wadi to the north to lie up for two hours in case our acquaintance might wish to introduce us to others.

Our next "arrivederci" was three days later. The air above was usually full of enough enemy aircraft to give us at least something to signal home about, but now at thirty feet a Fiat BR 20 bomber roared overhead and landed just below us half a mile away in a stretch of open plain. Orders were to keep quiet and undiscovered, but we knew that Headquarters, like Queen Bess, were not averse to privateering so long as it succeeded. The bomber was revving its engines angrily as if unable to take off. With two of my four trucks we circled around the hillside and drove across the plain with the sun, and wind, behind us. It was not very sporting, as it proved, for only one of the crew was manning a gun in the turret, and that jammed. At fifty yards range we stopped and opened fire. Three little men came out and we took them prisoner. I climbed into the aircraft and found the officer-pilot badly wounded, so we carried him out and put him on one of our trucks. A sergeant, manning the rear gun turret, was dead. We removed his body too. I took away all maps and papers. We poured petrol both inside and out and lit it with tracer-fire. It was important to wipe out traces of our crime if we were to remain undetected, for there were enemy garrisoning three posts, all within a few miles, and plenty of them in the sky, so we had to cart both dead and living away. The bombs started to explode just after we drew off and they very nearly brought down another Fiat bomber which circled low over its dying friend.

I decided we must take the wounded officer and three prisoners back west to LG 125, a hundred and eighty miles away. Very soon after we started the officer died. We had a sad little funeral ceremony as we buried him and the dead sergeant. The Patrol stood around the grave. I said a few prayers in English and withdrew to leave the three survivors to add some words in Italian before filling in the graves. It was neglect of my orders to leave Maaten el Grara, but we had to get these three prisoners back to the forward landing ground, nuisance though it was. Not that they behaved inconsiderately. Like most Italian prisoners they were the model of co-operation. When aircraft flew close by they would display their green uniforms while the rest of the Patrol hid under the trucks.

We reached the landing ground one and a half days later at the tail end of a succession of enemy air raids. Wing Commander Whiteley's Command had suffered heavy casualties, more in aircraft on the ground than in air crews. The three prisoners were sad to take leave of their guardsmen captors. From now on the more austere treatment normally accorded to prisoners of war was to be their lot. No more cigarettes when they wanted them, no more sleeping at night without even a guard to ensure their good behaviour.

That evening it was too late to replenish with petrol at the dump several miles away and start our journey back to Maaten el Grara. Moreover Wing Commander Whiteley asked me for our help in order to implement his commitments with "E" Force. The latter was now just outside Jalo about to attack it and waiting for the Wing at Landing Ground 125 to bomb the fort prior to the assault. The Wing was more than busy defending itself and could not provide air support for "E" Force. Worse still, wireless communication was not functioning between the two units. Whiteley could not inform Brigadier Reid that he must proceed with the attack without waiting for the promised bombers. During that night we made several attempts to get through to Siwa, but this was one of the rare instances when our own communications failed. There was too much signal traffic, even for us.

At dawn therefore I decided to split the Patrol into two halves.

Two trucks under Sergeant Penfold, including the wireless truck, were to return to Maaten el Grara, while I would proceed with two trucks to convey this extremely important message of Wing Commander Whiteley's to Brigadier Reid waiting near Jalo, one hundred and twenty miles away. Having done this I would rejoin the watch party. Barbour, our signaller, would transmit a message with this decision to Siwa as soon as he could get through.

After a few miles the truck accompanying mine gave much mechanical trouble, repeatedly delaying our urgent mission. Here I made the bad mistake of leaving it with Sergeant Penfold's party and the fitter, continuing to Jalo alone. At dawn the next morning, when 17 miles north of Jalo, the universal joint broke through my own incautious driving, I was stuck, so I had to continue to Jalo alone on foot.

It was a lonely feeling after I lost sight of my truck and its crew near some palm trees of a small uninhabited oasis, Jekerra. The sand was reasonably hard and even. I should, so I calculated, see the palm trees of Jalo ahead in about three hours. But "Was it still held by the enemy?" was my main worry. When near Jalo an armoured car appeared on the horizon and came towards me. It was South African, part of Reid's force.

Brigadier Reid had fortunately not waited long. He had attacked and taken Jalo that morning and the previous night, after a most successful assault by a battalion of Punjabis under Lieutenant Colonel Jenkins, supported to some extent by the armoured cars, though these had been difficult to use in the very soft sand of the oasis.

Jalo consists of a more or less rectangular oasis several miles in extent and includes three villages. The garrison of Italians had comprised about one thousand troops, now Brigadier Reid's prisoners. Three of these were preparing an excellent meal when I was brought to Force headquarters that evening. The Brigadier had rechristened them "Anthony", "James" and "William", after some show of protest at this uncatholic action. In civilian life they had been senior chefs at the best hotels in Rome, Geneva and Naples. In spite of my tardy arrival and the disgrace I knew myself to be in from the point of view of my own Headquarters, I was given most liberal hospitality. The wine bottles had been brought from the late Italian officers' mess, where they had at the time of the assault engaged the attention of the Italian officers more than their duties on the perimeter. Though deeply conscious that I was no more than a migrant bird fallen out of formation and much to be condemned by my companions still in flight, I spent a comfortable night inside a staff car, dressed in borrowed pullovers, coats and mufflers. Next morning I shaved with the Brigadier's razor.

At this exact date orders were being issued to all Patrols to raid the coastal road. It was not the moment to meet one's D-Day, with one's Patrol scattered over one hundred and fifty miles of desert. I being presumed lost by my Headquarters, Sergeant Penfold and his three trucks were ordered to search for me. They finally arrived at Jalo six days later. I had meanwhile got a message through to Siwa by "E" Force communications and Colonel Prendergast flew over from Siwa with the necessary spare parts for my truck and a restrained rocket for me. Here at Jalo we had been raided several times by enemy aircraft and a Blenheim had unfortunately been shot down by our own Ack Ack. Fearing therefore that the ultimate ignominy attached to my action would be to see my Commanding Officer shot down, I watched his arrival with trepidation, for his WACO aircraft closely resembled an Italian CR42 except for its lack of armament. But the chain of misfortunes was broken and, with the Patrol at last foregathered and my truck mended, we left for home at Siwa, arriving there four days before G.1 left for its next trip and five days before we ourselves went west again.

Beating up enemy communications was still the order of the day. The main battle in the north was going unfavourably: Rommel counter-attacked towards railhead and Army Headquarters. General Ritchie took over command from General Cunningham. Everything within our power must therefore be done to influence the indecisive state of the conflict.

After barely sufficient time for a rapid overhaul of their trucks and their wireless sets, G.1 under Captain Tony Hay set off to raid the Benghazi-Agedabia road again, leaving Siwa on 10 December. Near the road they met Captain Lloyd Owen with Y.2 Patrol. They bivouacked together for the night and discussed, beside the normal blazing camp fire, where each should make their attack. One of the best pleasures of the LRDG was the way one could usually light fires and keep warm after dark with impunity. Both the enemy and local natives would assume, at least in 1941, that the fire denoted no more than an Arab camp, while a unit with the main forces was obliged to exercise great care in so much as lighting a cigarette after dark.

The next day, in the afternoon, the Patrol attacked the road again, this time further north than a fortnight before. The previous raids, however, had disturbed the game which was now less plentiful. After some time a truck and staff car came along. These were duly destroyed. More waiting, but nothing more came, so the Patrol set off on a long night drive towards the south-east. It was intended to lie up for a while, allowing the enemy a little time to recover from this latest jab at his flank.

After changing course several times during the night to lose their tracks the Patrol arrived at dawn at a point near Maaten el Grara where G.2 and I had been a few days earlier and could see in the dim light of the rising sun a number of men walking about and a considerable quantity of mechanized transport, including British trucks of the familiar yellow colour. Before leaving Siwa the Patrol had been told that Brigadier Reid's "E" Force should be in the area of Agedabia by 12 December. It was now 16 December and Tony Hay naturally assumed that the men walking about were part of this British force. He and Sergeant Nolan went forward in the P/U to investigate. They drove straight into a large party of Germans.

The rest of the Patrol, according to Sergeant Roebuck, the senior survivor of the incident "were standing about and waiting for the P/U to return, and no one seemed to have any apprehension that the force in the wadi was other than British. Everything was peaceful until the P/U reappeared, driven in a most peculiar way, with the driver grinding the gearbox. The P/U then advanced towards us. Figures were seen to run to points on the hillside round us where they immediately opened fire. The P/U advanced towards us firing also, and was joined by other vehicles." Sergeant Roebuck then gave the order for the Patrol to withdraw, but unfortunately three of the trucks were too late to get away. They and their occupants became captives like Captain Hay and Sergeant Nolan. The remaining two trucks were chased for some distance, but finally escaped in spite of some damage to the vehicles. Without any proper navigational instruments they finally reached Siwa on 18 December. Ten men were captured with Captain Hay, nearly all picked men among the original members of "G" Patrol who had done the Murzuk trip and the operations of the previous summer. Thus their comrades lost, for the duration of the war, many good friends, and "G" Patrol many of its best exponents in the art of long-range patrolling.

Meanwhile, one day later than G.1's departure, the other half of the Patrol under my command left Siwa to destroy enemy traffic between Benghazi and Barce. There are two roads between these towns, one running near the coast by Tokra and the other inland via Benina and El Abiar. Alongside the latter road runs a railway. The country in this area is thickly populated and dotted with farms belonging to Italian colonists. I decided to attack this inland road and railway since they were the most approachable target. On such runs as this we considered all territory south of Trigh el Abd to be friendly ground, but once north of this one was in hostile territory. To avoid any possible repetition of a re-encounter with Tony Hay's JU 87 from Msus, we travelled across the open tract of country in the area of this post at night, arriving near the foothills of the Jebel in the early morning. On the way one truck touched a thermos bomb, but it did not explode.

As one approaches the Jebel from the south one looks up from the dry featureless plains to the rising tiers to the north, ridge upon ridge of hills, each more thickly covered with vegetation as they grow darker in the distance. After spending a long time in the flatness and lifelessness of the south one gazes at the shrubs and trees as though they were the garden of Eden. They reminded me of Europe and home. While the battle of Sidi Rezegh was raging to the east and the Junkers flew in their swarms overhead, it was impossible not to delight in the patches of green grass, the wild flowers that filled the small valleys, or the fields of young corn. On this particular trip we had perhaps too much opportunity to admire the scenery and with frequent wafts of wild thyme one became, like Ferdinand the Bull, inclined to wish the contest was less earnest.

The Ford 30-cwts with four-wheel drive performed amazing feats of mountaineering up and down the large boulders of the hillsides, twisting their chassis to negotiate the deep water courses. All the while natives sprang up from everywhere, Senussi shepherds, their wives and their children, offering "eggies" in return for Siwa dates. They had the knack of recognizing us as British instantly, though with our beards, our

40

unwashed faces and our diversity of clothing many of our compatriots would have disowned us.

For a day and a half we were completely stuck in the bottom of a deep wadi, for it came on to rain, making the red soil so slippery that we had to wait until the rain stopped. Such times were anxious ones, for we were within two to three miles of enemy garrisons and the native police who patrolled these regions could easily report our presence. The aircraft overhead were foiled by plenty of camouflage. We rubbed our trucks over with a mixture of the local red soil and engine oil and decked them with branches of trees. For the best part of a day we kept watch on the El Abiar road and railway, but hardly a movement was seen. Plans were therefore made to make a raid on the far coastal road near Tokra. These were, unluckily perhaps, never fulfilled.

My soldier servant, Wann, was extremely ill; he had a very high temperature and great pain in the stomach. These symptoms were transmitted to Siwa for medical advice. Numerous messages and recipes for treatment were passed on this subject and I suggested to the Commanding Officer, by W/T, splitting the Patrol, leaving the two trucks with Wann and continuing with the other two. This was, however, vetoed and I was instructed to bring Wann, now very seriously ill, to Landing Ground 125, the forward landing ground described earlier.

We had a somewhat eventful journey back. In the afternoon of 18 December we watched Benghazi being bombed by the RAF and then some ME 109s chasing our bombers away. That evening, travelling south, our attention was engaged by the sight of lights to the east, first two or three in the dusk, then more and more, finally hundreds, coming towards us across the eastern horizon. It was obviously a force of very considerable size, impossible to say what nationality. As we drove on south, stopping to watch now and then, many of the lighted vehicles passed us, and still more kept coming on. According to the BBC news report the Battle of Sidi Rezegh was still raging and indecisive. Aircraft were overhead dropping a few flares and bombs and raiding Msus just to the west. It must be Rommel in retreat! For two hours we tried to get through to Siwa to pass on the red-hot news. With all these enemy vehicles milling round, we felt that no newspaper reporter sending a despatch could have been more on the spot. About one in the morning many of them stopped, and for us, travelling without lights, it was necessary to take care not to tread on the tail of a sleeping tank. We passed near plenty of dormant shapes and saw one or two of their tanks and armoured cars at dawn near the Trigh el Abd, but they went on sleeping.

We met some of our own armoured cars on approaching LG 125, who mistook us for enemy tanks and fled with the west wind. They stopped eventually and we had to exercise some care to avoid a civil war. We dropped Wann at the landing ground whence he was flown to Jarabub by one of our WACOs. His illness turned out to be not appendicitis, as we thought, but malignant malaria. Here at Landing Ground 125 we heard of G.1's disaster. We were given orders for a fresh operation which were then cancelled, owing to the rapid advance of 8th Army. Finally we were recalled to Siwa, reaching there at teatime on 21 December.

Chapter Three

INTERLUDE AT EL AGHEILA

Rommel crossed back into Tripolitania on 6 January 1942. 8th Army closed up: its objective was still to continue the advance to Tripoli, but the prolonged fighting in "Crusader" had used up a lot of resources and a pause for a logistic build-up was necessary. But now the intervention of Japan in the Far East caused diversion of resources and reinforcements on which Auchinleck had been relying for the continuation of his advance.

Meanwhile Rommel had acquired shorter lines of communication and had no intention of being pushed back to Tripoli.

In this short pause before the next round the LRDG participated in major SAS raids. Their areas of penetration were moved forward well into Tripolitania, but this was not to last long.

When we had been at Siwa before, the Patrol had lived among the palm trees of the oasis, using the redundant truck tarpaulins as shelters against heat and occasional rain, with mosquito nets rigged across them to reduce the number of flies. We now moved into better quarters, plaster and stone buildings. Much though I love pomegranates and palm trees, with their streams and pools, I know that soldiers must give priority to efficiency and familiarity in selecting a base to work from. What is practical is better than what is picturesque. We did our best to get the wireless truck back from overhaul as soon as possible so that the civilian short-wave set could play and talk close by one of the windows, and even the navigator would forget all about checking his chronometer by the Greenwich time signal. And if one could avoid sending all the Patrol's trucks for overhaul at workshops at the same time, some were then available as sources of electricity supply, their inspection lamps dangling through the windows.

The greatest blessing from the move out of the palm trees to the stone buildings three hundred yards across the small landing ground was the escape from mosquitoes. The previous summer all Patrols based on Siwa had suffered badly from malaria. On descending the main track down the escarpment into Siwa from Mersa Matruh, a notice read: "You are entering a mosquito-infested area". And so it was in the summer of 1941, just before I joined. The Headquarters buildings on a small hill housed the Commanding Officer, the Signal Section and a large part of Headquarters personnel. They had been all right. The buildings of the local inhabitants were mostly away from the palm trees.

The answer was that mosquitoes are lazy fliers. They don't like taking off into the wind, usually to the south-west at Siwa. Nor do they like to fly far. So the summer of 1942, much later than this part of the story, was almost free of malaria. We took our mepacrin tablets, but they were only a postponement remedy and now I think they were not really needed.

Robin Gurdon and I, for the short three-month period when we served together, had a small building to ourselves: a bedroom each and a sitting room between, quite comfortable until my green canvas and wood collapsible arm chair collapsed under the weight of Randolph Churchill. I was away at the time, in May 1942. He had been a member of David Stirling's audacious party into Benghazi, spending two nights and a day in an attempt to clamp magnetic mines on the shipping in the harbour. It was ruined by leaks in the folboats. Fitzroy Maclean, another member of the party, foiled the sentries in the dark, passing himself off as a short-tempered Italian officer. Robin Gurdon's G.2 Patrol provided the transport (except for Stirling's "blitz-wagon"). My broken chair marked the end of a frustrating but remarkable journey. I had to recognize that Robin's lack of real sympathy for my loss was understandable, after he had finished with his story. To claim, as I had, that the Germans had suffered much less than I had from the SAS latest action was not in fair perspective.

But that was later on – in May. Now, back to Christmas 1941, which was celebrated as well as limited circumstances allowed. There was a very small ration of beer, but rum was, as usual, the main contributor to such elation as we could achieve. The Commanding Officer went round Patrols to remind us of what we were missing at home and what we were fighting for. Yet the festivity could not be lively, for there were other matters in hand. Most of Christmas had to be spent loading trucks and filling ammunition belts and magazines. Deserted private belongings and kit-bags stood around. Though the majority of "G" Patrol was still here, it was lonely without the eleven from G.1 who had been captured near Agedabia and whose fate was uncertain. At dawn on the 26th G.2 had to leave for the far west.

Before starting with G.2 Patrol under my command for the Misurata-Hon road, some of the work of the other Patrols must be summarized. Such references as these are not intended to be complete, but they give a picture of the activities of the Group as a whole. They also draw attention to the highly successful early raids by the SAS, transported and helped by our Patrols, on enemy landing grounds near the Cyrenaica-Tripolitania border.

By the middle of December "A" Squadron with the two Rhodesian patrols (S.1 and S.2) and a New Zealand Patrol (T.2) were sent to Jalo to come under the command of Brigadier Reid and "E" Force for a few weeks (where I had been shortly before). The Rhodesian patrols took parties of SAS to raid the landing grounds near Tamet. Stirling and Mayne destroyed twenty-four aircraft. At Agedabia the SAS party under Fraser destroyed thirty-seven aircraft, making a total of seventy-seven for one night. On 24 December S.1 under Gus Holliman took further SAS parties to Sirte and Tamet again, and on Christmas Day T.2, under Captain Morris, who had carried out a daring and successful raid at Mersa Brega shortly before, took Jock Lewes (Welsh Guards – SAS) and Fraser and their SAS parties to Nofilia and Ras Lanouf (Marble Arch) landing grounds.

These raids by "L" Detachment SAS comprised the first of their really spectacular achievements. As was the case with the first raids by LRDG Patrols on the main coastal road, these attacks on aerodromes found the enemy unprepared for such sudden action in areas so far behind their main forces. To start with their aircraft were not very widely dispersed and the

45

defences of the landing grounds ill prepared. But soon it became much more difficult to repeat the first successful actions. Yet, in spite of the enemy's increasing precautions, the SAS continued to deplete the enemy's aircraft on the ground in whatever part of Libya they might be.

It was on the Ras Lanouf operation that Lieutenant Jock Lewes was killed. He had been the mainspring in the early days of training of "L" Detachment. His ingenuity had been responsible for much of their equipment and tactics and he had himself set the highest example of resourcefulness and determination which became a pattern for all members of that unit until the close of their operations in Libya a year later, and even afterwards in other lands to which the scene of hostilities shifted.

Lewes was killed when T.2 Patrol was on its way to collect the party of SAS dropped at Marble Arch. They were attacked first by a Messerschmitt, then by two Stukas and then by more, which maintained a continuous strafing of the Patrol and their trucks throughout the rest of the day. During the attack the trucks became widely separated and, although Morris himself and some of his Patrol were able to get back to Jalo on the one surviving vehicle, nine LRDG men and one parachutist found themselves that evening the best part of 200 miles from their base at Jalo. Their total resources were three gallons of water, one packet of biscuits, one emergency ration, a compass and a map of the eastern part of the area. They then set out on a journey which in endurance fell little if anything short of the long march of the four men who walked from near Kufra towards the Chad the previous spring, known as "Moore's March", described in Michael Crichton Stuart's book *G Patrol*.

The whole story cannot be told here, but, in brief, after walking more than 200 miles in eight days they all reached Aujila near Jalo, except the parachutist who, with his feet almost raw, had been obliged to fall out near the El Agheila-Marada road. Half way along their route they had come upon some Arabs who had given them some dates and water and sheltered them for a night. They suffered much from the cold, being forced to walk at night and to rest by day, and also from their footwear falling to pieces on the rough going. One man arrived at Aujila wearing a piece cut from a greatcoat on one foot and part of the canvas carrier of a Lewis gun magazine on the other.

At a far less heroic level, it was about this time (16 December) that the LRDG's modest Artillery Section's operation took place. A fairly isolated fort in the area south of Agedabia was selected as the target. A force comprising the 25-pounder gun mounted on a 10-ton Mack lorry and a Rhodesian Patrol (S.2) first reconnoitred the fort, which was found to be standing in a hollow and in a poor state of repair, and then took up positions around it. At zero hour, 1630 hours, the 25-pounder opened fire. It fired, in all, fourteen shells. This brought four Italian soldiers running out of the fort who were duly captured. The fort itself was found to be empty and very little of value was discovered among its contents, except that the prisoners were glad to retrieve their personal belongings and blankets before being led into captivity.

On 20 December three Patrols, mostly New Zealanders, accompanied 22nd Guards Brigade, included in Bencol under Brigadier Marriott, in their advance across the desert towards the coast south of Benghazi.

Another Patrol was sent to carry out a liaison task with Leclerc's Free French Forces at Zouar, south of the Tibesti, with very premature optimism. It was hoped that the French forces would advance northward into Tripolitania and thereby contribute towards the offensive which at this time was contemplated against the enemy forces in eastern Tripolitania. This phase of operations did not materialize until a year later when 8th Army under Montgomery made its third and successful attempt to reach Tripoli.

At this stage a new set of operations for LRDG Patrols was issued. 8th Army had driven Rommel out of Cyrenaica and reserves and supplies were being brought up to continue the advance westwards into Tripolitania.

Agedabia had been taken; there was talk of taking Marada, and the next bounds would be El Agheila, Sirte, Buerat el Hosn and beyond.

Our orders from 8th Army were:-

1   "To carry out offensive patrols as far back behind enemy lines as possible, and to act aggressively against enemy communications etc., in areas where such action is unlikely to be expected.

2   In the course of movement across Tripolitania Patrols will make note of topographical details that may be of

assistance to the subsequent advance of other troops through the area.

3   In addition, Patrols will watch out for and report enemy movements and will indicate as soon as possible whether there are any signs of a position being prepared in the area of Buerat."

To conform with these orders the LRDG divided up the northern part of Tripolitania from El Agheila to Tripoli in well-defined areas. Patrols were to be allotted to each area and there they would cause maximum possible damage to enemy communications, and also report on the state of the going, on geographical obstacles and on enemy movements and dispositions in the course of their offensive activities.

With most of the Group still at Siwa and some at Jalo, these areas presented enormous problems of distance. To go beyond the Buerat el Hosn road we had to cover over 750 miles from Siwa with no forward dumps beyond Jalo. Moreover, the only means of approach into this area was far more restricted than the method of access to all regions of Cyrenaica. Patrols could fan out there from the area of Jarabub in a variety of directions and make direct for any point on the circumference of Cyrenaica. To approach the area of Sirte it was necessary to cross the 100-mile gap between Marada and El Agheila, now on the line of the enemy's forward defences. The country south of Marada was not thought practicable. It had been scantily investigated and contained indeterminate sand seas, escarpments and mountains which were known to be extremely difficult, if not impassable. A reconnaissance in this area by the "Marada Patrol" of Captain Crichton Stuart is described in his book *G Patrol*. The mountains which started about forty miles inland from the sea forced Patrols which had crossed the Marada-El Agheila road to keep close to the coast and to the now much-used enemy landing grounds, Merduma, Nofilia, Sirte, Tamet and Buerat. Once beyond Sirte formidable obstacles would be encountered: the deep wadis of Tamet, Zem Zem and Sofeggin and then the succession of escarpments and deep ravines which lead to the plateau of Mizda, south of Tripoli.

The day before Christmas Captain Lloyd Owen with Y.2 left to carry out offensive action in his allotted area. This operation remained for many months to come as marking the furthest penetration westward by our forces. Two days later, on 26 December, G.2 and I left Siwa for an area adjoining Lloyd Owen's on the east, that is covering the Buerat el Hosn/Bu Ngem area and the district south-east of Misurata. This would entail operating over 750 miles west of Siwa, yet it made one feel in some respects near home to be concerned with a meridian nearer to Greenwich than to Cairo. We had a good deal of mechanical difficulty just after leaving Siwa which was put right for a while by a workshop in Jarabub. Here, too, Guardsman Murray had to be left at the MDS and Corporal Stocker had his only tooth extracted at the Dressing Station, not the workshop.

At Jalo two of the trucks had their engines changed and here Hogmanay was spent in the company of some of "A" Squadron and a curious small unit which had turned up. This consisted of three Officers and six Other Ranks with three magnificently equipped Ford cars. They were under the command of Pilot Officer Rawnsley, the other two officers being Lieutenant John Pearson-Gregory (Grenadier Guards) and a Naval Lieutenant-Commander submariner with a DSO. Derek Rawnsley said their job was to reconnoitre sites of prospective new airfields towards Tripoli. Pearson-Gregory stated that they were there to beat up whatever they saw. The submariner said he was there as navigator, on holiday, home from the sea. As we had divided up the country westward into clearly defined sections in order that each Patrol would not be disturbed by the activities of another, it was felt that Rawnsley's party was likely to be more of a nuisance to us than to the enemy. It was obvious that when a Patrol is carrying out a raid or disturbs the enemy their reaction will make the area unsafe for others. Luckily for us Rawnsley had not sufficient petrol to go further. After I had communicated my feelings to HQ at Siwa, this more-or-less RAF ground force was called off our hunting ground.

Nevertheless we all sat down happily together on New Year's Eve to do what we could by way of celebration under a Jalo palm tree. It came on to rain and went on raining throughout the night, but the fire round which we sat and the burning elements in the punch we consumed made us oblivious to any such discomfort. Corporal Fraser (later Sergeant) had concocted a devastating brew. Into the rum was put anything he could find. On being asked what the ingredients were, he replied that he could not possibly remember except that there were some eggs and dates and sugar. The naval officer had an immense fund of stories and Rawnsley's songs from RAF sources provided novelties unknown to us too. The party broke up, as parties do, in the best tradition of a Hogmanay night, but with little forethought for the earnest prospects of the morrow.

By orders given out before the party began, the Patrol was to leave early. At 8 o'clock, in fact, the Patrol moved out of the oasis and headed past the small oasis of Aujila for the west. The travelling was easy and the drivers drove mechanically on, nor did anything occur which might have required arousing the gunners. We crossed the Marada-El Agheila road at dusk the next day after sighting an occasional aircraft, and a truck passed us in the dark, a short distance away, heading eastwards. It was an eerie sight and seemed to shy away from us. This was, so we heard later, the only surviving truck of T.2 Patrol (Morris) which had been badly shot up by enemy aircraft, as already related.

After moonrise we continued north-west in the early hours of the morning and drove on until an hour after dawn on good going north of the hills. There was very little cover, but we tucked up into some small hollows, well dispersed and camouflaged, and had breakfast. As soon as we switched off our engines we could hear the noise of aircraft. There were two ME 109s circling slowly, about a mile away. They were exactly on the line of our route until I turned left on some hard going. We were now at the entrance to Tripolitania between the extensive salt marshes by the coast and the inland hills. Here the enemy was obviously maintaining a conscientious air patrol to stop the bottleneck and prevent a re-occurrence of the recent raids near Sirte, Nofilia and Tamet, including the one of the night before which we did not yet know about. All that day these two aircraft and others who relieved them at intervals circled round and above us, sometimes passing barely a hundred yards away. Darkness fell at last and I decided to put as big a distance as possible between ourselves and this uncomfortable area.

We drove all night long, covering a hundred miles. My eyes were dizzy by dawn with peering into the darkness. We had stopped only once, at 2am, to light a good fire to warm us and to provide a hot brew of tea. An aircraft was seen when we were having breakfast after dawn, so that, feeling by now somewhat "aircraft happy", especially on hearing the news by wireless of T.2's troubles, we set off westward keeping well to the south along the hills, where there was some cover, and not too near the coastal strip with its aerodromes.

In our previous trip to Barce our old Fords had proved themselves as good as chamois in the art of mountaineering, and here again we taxed their skill in negotiating impossible gradients and boulder-strewn river beds. In this country one would go along quite happily for a mile or two on hard black gravel only to reach a gaping chasm where the wadis had their origin.

After three days of this we clambered down the steep sides of a gorge, made our way all morning past the boulders and tamarisk trees along the bottom, and finally emerged into an open plain of soft sand with a thin black gravel surface, crossed by a long barrier of sand dunes. At the eastern end of the plain runs the Hon-Misurata road and near this point lies a succession of old forts looking down on it. I had decided on this area for our first raid or ambush. There were plenty of fresh tracks on the semi-metalled road and it was impossible to know whether the forts were garrisoned or not. An ascent was made to the nearest fort, which our party conducted with all the tenseness and the precautions which a raiding force of Goths would have shown had they assaulted the citadel of Rome a second time, only to find no occupant, no Italian soldier, no goose.

An ambush was prepared beside the road where it made several bends through a small rise in the ground. The trucks were parked fifty yards away from it, on the same side, and camouflaged. Mines were laid on the tracks we had made in pulling off the road, as a precaution against pursuing tanks. About two hundred yards of the highway were covered by machine guns, dismounted from the trucks and set up by the road's edge. Both above and below our position mines were placed on the verges, while holes were hacked in the surface and then lightly filled in, so that the mines could be placed quickly in position in case of pursuit in either direction.

All was quiet that night while the moon glistened on the walls and towers of the old Roman fort above us. The next day, after an aircraft flying low had passed down the line of the road, a large Diesel came along. We duly let fly at it when it came opposite us. It pulled off the road, riddled with bullets, and the driver was extracted faint with fear, bowed but unbloody. He gave us rather unwillingly some information about enemy garrisons in the neighbourhood, and was not nearly such an agreeable companion as our previous Italian captives. We had unfortunately missed by a few hours a good-sized convoy which passed south the day before. Nothing more came by that day.

At dawn the next day another large lorry came along from the north. At first its sounds were mistaken for an aircraft and everyone kept under the trucks, and then, on realizing that a potential victim was heading for the trap, we came running out to man the guns. Some of us must have been seen, for the lorry stopped just short of our position and the premature firing of one of our guns gave the show away. The lorry contained about a dozen native troops, most of whom jumped out and started to fire back, while the driver turned the lorry around. Before they got away some of us closed in with Tommy guns and hit quite a number, later discovered to include six killed.

The lorry had forty-five miles to cover to return to Bu Ngem, the nearest sizeable garrison. At the speed it was going it would cover this in less than one and a half hours. Pursuit was out of the question as our trucks were camouflaged and it would take some time to get moving. As the enemy had aircraft on the landing ground at Bu Ngem they were bound to be after us in the air in about two hours. So we laid the mines in the road, drove down it to where we had first met it, and followed our very conspicuous tracks across the plain towards the hills.

In whatever direction we went, our tracks were bound to show up white against the black gravel surface and it seemed best to double back on our original tracks and then turn off them as soon as we came to hard going. After some anxious sticks in the soft line of dunes we reached the hills with their clumps of tamarisk and bushes; then, keeping to some hard rock, we turned away from our old tracks and went up a wadi towards the north.

We had just time to disperse the trucks at several-hundred-yard intervals and camouflage them more carefully than we had ever done before when enemy aircraft arrived exactly at the end of two hours. They came, three of them, Savoias, roaring along our conspicuous tracks across the plain. They then, as we had hoped, followed along the wadi where we had originally come from and did not appear to notice where we had turned off. We could see them having some trouble in following our old tracks, especially in the deeper gorges towards the high hills. They circled back towards us at times. We thought we had at last eluded them on hearing them drop all their bombs among some inoffensive bushes up a wadi where we had formerly been. They apparently took an hour off for lunch and during this interlude they must have thought out more carefully our probable action and come to the conclusion that it had been impossible for us to travel more than a very short distance from the scene of the ambush before they had appeared. As a result they plotted our probable position only too accurately. They came straight for our area and circled round endlessly. At times they would drop their bombs into a clump of bushes, making shallow dives around and above us all the while. Still, somehow our trucks were not seen. They had been placed away from all bushes, close to the wadi sides and made to resemble part of their rocky slopes.

It was an anxious day from 10 in the morning till 4.30 pm, lying under the trucks or near them, praying against an expected burst of bullets which might ignite our vehicles with their large loads of petrol, and also against the arrival of a ground force that might be sent out to track us down. With only four trucks and twelve men very widely dispersed an attack from a ground force would have been difficult to deal with. It is in fact the combination of an attack from the ground and from the air that provides the material for a Patrol commander's worst nightmare. Aircraft make one take cover without regard to the ground defence, whereas a reasonable defensive position, with trucks leaguered close together, would be easily spotted from the air.

Night fell at last and the enemy aircraft went home. We made off towards the north using our lights as little as possible, over very difficult country. When the moon rose we could see our way a little better through the morass of escarpments, plateaux and deep wadis. We were going north for two reasons. First, I wanted to raid the main North Road between Buerat and Misurata. The engines of our trucks, it is true, were old and consuming inordinate quantities of oil, but I calculated that we had just sufficient petrol to reach the nearest point on the road and get nearly all the way home hoping to acquire additional petrol and oil in the course of a successful raid. Secondly, though we could not cover much distance from the scene of the previous day's events in one night owing to the difficult country, yet it was possible at least to go in an unexpected direction. By going north, and thereby passing close to the garrison at Bu Ngem, we might avoid any further search in the direction in which the enemy most expected us to go, namely east or south-east.

The next day we again had much mechanical trouble with the vehicles and lay up to carry out such repairs as we could. Meanwhile we could hear in the distance the buzzing of aircraft searching to our south, as we had expected, but they never came to trouble us where we were. After continuing north in the evening over more bad going, I finally decided to abandon the proposed raid on the main road and turn for home, to Jalo, 500 miles away. The petrol supply was now very low and the oil situation even worse; the valuable wireless truck had run a little end and was never satisfied with its ration of oil.

We travelled eastward, taking the risk of keeping nearer the coast on the good, though very open, going. One or two aircraft were seen, but the eyesight of our fitter, Scott, was quite phenomenal: he could see aircraft very far away, before they were likely to see us, so that we could halt in an undulation or against the best background available until the danger had passed. Our standard practice was that all trucks stopped when one of them stopped. Our dust was usually more conspicuous from the air than our trucks. "Scott's truck has stopped, Sir," I would often be told by Wann or another member of my crew. Scott would be pointing in the direction of an aircraft. When we switched off our engines we could usually hear it, but not always see it. We must have been saved from many nasty encounters by Scott, an Anglo-Indian, patient, calm and with a great dexterity as a fitter. I would leave him alone to work when he had a problem. Usually I would lie under my own truck reading *The Idiot* (Dostoevsky) or *War and Peace* until I got a message from Scott that we could move on.

We crossed the deep Wadi Tamet well to the north where it flattens out before reaching the sea, then, further east all night, making for the Marada-El Agheila road. Headquarters instructed us at dawn call-time to try to return south of Marada owing to increasing defence preparations by the enemy between Marada and the sea, and so we headed south-east instead of east-south-east. Before turning towards the jagged hills and escarpments near Marada we were circled by a ME 110, but it must have taken us for Germans. A CR 42 zig-zagged by at 100 feet; he must have been blind.

The country through which we now had to travel was more fantastic than anything I had experienced before. There

54

were successions of abrupt escarpments with deep soft hollows at their feet, white and yellow and purple, and then over to the south-east, black jagged hills like the spires of cathedrals and narrow defiles, which we passed through, resembling the streets of a mediaeval city. Ribs of white rock, filled in with soft pulverized limestone, shook the trucks until they groaned and gasped and squeaked and cried out for still more oil. But we had no more. We took all the oil from the guns' tool-kits and out of the rifle butts. We extracted as much as we dared from each differential casing. This provided us with a new quota of oil of doubtful quality. To take the nearest line for home we cut the corner close round Marada. Travelling across some excellent sand sheet at last, the beginning of the big dunes, with black sentinels of rock rising here and there, we could see the palm trees of Marada on our left which shaded a German garrison.

Stretching east from Marada was a deep valley lined with palm trees reaching to the complicated depression round Ain Sidi Mohammed, fifty miles away. To the north it was bounded by a great escarpment and to the south, as we soon discovered, by the worst sand seas I have ever met. Going into it from the south-west it seemed innocent enough to start with. We were making for the deep valley just mentioned and the scattered line of dunes we first encountered seemed to meet us like a succession of gigantic bobsleigh tracks pointing in the right direction. Avoiding the troughs and banking up on the sides where it was hard, it was exciting, fast and enjoyable, and then there came a dead end, definitely no thoroughfare. We dug our way through this and promptly met another dune barrier. Any truck which succeeded in advancing a few hundred yards would be followed by the rest. Within half a mile of the valley we were aiming for all the trucks found themselves finally in a small hollow of sand. Try as they might they could not get out either backwards or forwards. It seemed as if we would have to start taking the trucks to pieces, carrying them the last stretch and reassembling them on the hard sand in the bottom of the valley.

After emptying them of all their loads, however, we finally pulled and pushed and tugged them through, using all the sand mats and sand channels as we devoted our attention to each truck in turn. The loads were manhandled and were replaced in the trucks after two days' exertion. A Savoia on regular patrol used to fly over us but never took any notice, and in the valley could be seen the fresh tracks of a sizeable enemy patrol which presumably we might meet on our way towards Ain Sidi Mohammed. The depression here had mud flats and very complicated structures of dunes on its southern edge. In this we became unpleasantly involved and here poor No. 6 truck reached its last resting place. Its engine had seized through lack of oil, for it had given too much of its life blood away in sustaining the more valuable wireless truck. We removed its contents and bade it farewell, expecting never to see it again in this remote dune-covered area. Four months later, however, it acquired a fascination which brought us back again – it had what other trucks had not got, five good tyres which saved us from ruin on another long-distance trip the following May.

After sticking in the salt marsh and finally crossing the edge of it with the anxiety of one skating on very thin ice, we reached a point in the escarpment to the north where we could surmount it, and from thence on to Aujila and Jalo by the hard, beautiful gravel and sand plain. To cross these undulating strips of good going gives a sensation of the smooth, high speed of an aeroplane. When you come into Jalo from the south it is much like landing at an aerodrome, for the sand in the oasis is very soft, and one circles round to come in from the open desert on the hard going far out from the trees before making one's run into the selected point of access.

We reached Jalo on 18 January 1942, three days before the Afrika Korps launched its counter-offensive, about a year after its first attempt. Our commanders who had been planning for 8th Army to go further west had got it all wrong.

Chapter Four

ROMMEL STRIKES BACK

*The transfer of Kesselring's Luftflotte 2 from Russia
had weakened the ability of our Malta-based forces to
stop Axis convoys reaching Libya, and Rommel's
supply position had greatly improved. On 21 January
1942 he struck at 8ᵗʰ Army's forward positions east of
El Agheila on the Tripolitanian border.*

*8ᵗʰ Army (now under General Neil Ritchie who had
replaced General Cunningham) was "off-balance"
and had lost some formations to the Far Eastern theatre
after Japan had declared war. After some serious
reverses, and failures of command, 8ᵗʰ Army retreated
from Benghazi and Western Cyrenaica, and started to
fortify a line stretching from Gazala near the coast
to Bir Hakeim 45 miles to the south. Rommel, who had
his own logistic problems, closed up slowly.*

*The LRDG was forced to withdraw from its new
forward base at Jalo oasis to Kufra and Siwa in order
to continue its support of 8ᵗʰ Army.*

After Tony Hay's capture, I was the only officer left in Guards
Patrol. G.1 was now sadly depleted. Some men were transferred
from my half of the Patrol, and a few recently attached to Group
HQ were called back. G.1 was thus restored sufficiently to take
the field once more. Captain A.D.N. Hunter, Royal Scots
Fusiliers, who normally commanded one of the Yeomanry
Patrols, was placed in temporary command, and their task was
to convey a party of "L" Detachment SAS and folboatists under
David Stirling to Buerat el Hosn. This small locality came into
prominence at this time since it was supposed (quite wrongly)
that the enemy were organizing a defensive line there. It
comprised a small port and jetty, a wireless station, a vehicle

park and landing ground reported much used as a staging area for reserves of aircraft on their way forward. Such installations presented, if this information was correct, a target deserving SAS attention.

The Patrol left Jalo on 16 January, two days before G.2 Patrol and I returned from the trip just described. As the narrow entrance into Tripolitania north of Marada was now considered unsafe, they were obliged to go round by the south. They therefore set a course which swung far to the south of where I had just been, hoping to find a route through the patches of complicated sand sea in that area and penetrate the southern flank of the mountains at a point further west than G.2 had come through, or than the line which Captain Crichton Stuart had taken the year before. In this they succeeded. They met a large escarpment near the start, crossed curious belts of dunes and surmounted the hills south of Sirte where the going was difficult but better than any experienced in this region before.

At about this time several other Patrols made passages through this area on roughly the same route as that taken by Captain Hunter; and thus a considerable amount of information was soon gained, enabling the Group's Intelligence Officer to supply a recommended itinerary for later Patrols. Variations of this route proved extremely valuable later in order to maintain a road watch near El Agheila by Patrols operating from Kufra, and still later when the tide of battle swung west again with Montgomery, and large numbers of SAS and LRDG were once more intensively engaged in Tripolitania.

To return to Captain Hunter, the Patrol emerged into the coastal plain and from now on tried to travel by night as a result of enemy aircraft activity. They spent much time in descending into Wadi Tamet, and at dawn were spotted by reconnaissance aircraft. The trucks were tucked away in small crevices and the crews ordered to keep clear of them. Enemy aircraft bombed such trucks as they saw intermittently all day, but only succeeded in destroying one. In the afternoon when the Patrol reassembled it was found that three men, Guardsmen Smith and Anderson and the wireless operator, were missing (I learnt later that they survived as POWs). The Patrol waited for some time but had to continue in the early hours of the morning when the moon rose, as the operation was urgent and delay had been incurred in overcoming the geographical difficulties encountered. Beyond Wadi Tamet more bad going was met with, but the Patrol finally reached a hiding place suitable as a base for operations 25 miles south of Buerat.

The loss of the signaller was serious. Captain Stirling had arranged for last-moment information to be sent him regarding enemy aircraft movements. The latest report before leaving stated that no substantial numbers were on the landing ground, and Stirling therefore did not attack it, though, in fact, a large number had arrived two days before. He drove down the main road outside Buerat finding little traffic, for it was after dark. Time bombs were placed in a few vehicles by the roadside and an entry was made into a guarded vehicle park. The sentries here were not very vigilant and one of them even helped a member of the raiding party to negotiate some barbed wire, mistaking him for one of his own officers. Time bombs were duly placed in some twenty-three trucks, and these, as well as those on the road, soon went up in loud explosions. On the way back the truck containing the party, driven by Guardsman Gibson, was ambushed. On the outward journey a post of Italian soldiers had not been observed, nor had the enemy shown any active interest. On the way back, however, it was soon clear that news of the raid had been passed on. The enemy had placed machine guns on the verge of the road and were awaiting the raiders' return. They opened up as the truck approached, but Gibson drove straight on, charging through anyone standing on the road, while an SAS gunner made good use of a machine gun, blazing away into the enemy as the truck passed through. The enemy fire was ill-directed and the whole party ran the gauntlet unscathed. Meanwhile a party of folboatists had raided the wireless station near the shore. Whilst they were waiting to be picked up by one of our trucks they watched enemy dive-bombers swooping down and bombing the beach nearby, probably thinking they saw our men on the sea shore awaiting a rendezvous with a submarine. This party too was picked up and brought back to the rendezvous.

In returning homeward the Patrol took care to avoid the bad going towards the south and kept to the hard flat country near the coast, as G.2 had done, luckily without interference by enemy aircraft. They then turned south round Marada by much the same way as we had come, and arrived at Jalo on 31 January, little knowing, through lack of wireless communication, that

Rommel's counter-offensive had pushed the 8th Army back to Mekili (150 miles NE of Agedabia) by this time.

During January most of the LRDG, including Group Headquarters, had been concentrated at Jalo as a base for operations, (under the illusion that we were going further west). Some Patrols were being sent back in rotation to Cairo to refit. On 21 January Rommel's counter-attack broke through Agedabia. Msus, 8th Army's forward supply centre, was captured on the 24th. The 1st Armoured Division, comprising most of our forward units, proceeded to withdraw somewhat hastily past Cheruba and Mekili. So far as we were concerned, information about the confused state of affairs in the north was scanty at first.

The Heavy Transport Section, which had left Cairo a few weeks before, had gone to Kufra, whence it had brought additional supplies to Jalo. It was now sent off to Tobruk, our new supply head. Through the skill of its commander it got through with impunity. Then, not being able to return to Jalo, it proceeded to Siwa, completing a 3400-mile journey. Less fortunate was a small supply column under the Adjutant sent to Msus to draw ammunition and mail. It was waylaid and captured by some German Mark IIIs, with the exception of a few of our men who succeeded in bolting on foot, found an abandoned Crusader tank and drove in it to safety. Hoping, however, that the influx of Germans to our north would soon be checked and even repulsed, preparations were at first made for only tentative evacuation of our base at Jalo. We had brought up, in the prevailing optimism, large quantities of supplies to be able to transport them in the vehicles we had with us. A point at the edge of the Sand Sea, Chetmir, about 15 miles away, was chosen as a temporary HQ under our 2nd in Command, Eric Wilson. A ferry service was instituted to transfer our more important stores there. G.2 Patrol, under myself, was left to guard the oasis.

It soon became evident, however, that events near the coast had taken a more permanent turn for the worse, and the LRDG was obliged to withdraw to its old bases at Siwa and Kufra. The majority of the Patrols, together with Group Headquarters, retired therefore to Siwa. As much of our stores as possible were taken there, leaving a considerable quantity at Chetmir, the temporary halting place at the edge of the Great Sand Sea.

With G.2 I was now left alone at Jalo to carry out the task, first, of demolishing all remaining stores and ammunition dumps, and secondly to await the arrival of Hunter and Stirling with G.1, who, having no wireless communication, would be ignorant of the new state of affairs.

Most of our old stores had been removed and the material to be destroyed consisted almost entirely of enemy bomb and ammunition dumps and semi-derelict vehicles. The area of Jalo is extensive. It was difficult therefore to take adequate precautions against the sudden appearance of an enemy force and at the same time to carry out the demolitions. Moreover it might be necessary to wait here for ten days before the arrival of G.1, assuming it was still alive – and their wireless silence was ominous. In the meantime, therefore, this second task had to be neglected in order to concentrate on the business of our scorched earth, or "scorched palm", policy.

Next to the inner landing ground were numerous piles of old Italian ammunition. Each of these was stacked and closely packed with bits of wood. Aviation petrol, of which there was a surplus, was poured on to several of these at a time, and one would then fire tracer to ignite them. Another method of destroying ammunition dumps, and this was the most successful method practised on a dump of aircraft bombs, was merely to pack each dump with the contents of cases of gelignite, which was also expendable, and then detonate the charge with fuse and primer. A slowly-burning dump of ammunition makes a very fair representation of a battle at its height. First the small arms ammunition provides the semblance of a brisk exchange of machine-gun fire; then the 20 mm ammunition, followed by the 47 mm shells, high explosive, armour-piercing and star shells, add to the crescendo which reaches its height when the large shells and bombs explode, as though the Navy and Air Force have joined in Armageddon on the ground. Drums of burning diesel oil sent pillars of black smoke into the sky, stretching long arms away to the horizon. Day and night for nearly a week the crackle, thunder, flame and smoke continued. At first a few messages from our Headquarters, who were some miles away withdrawing eastward, asked anxiously after our well-being, fearing that we were the victims of an onslaught of a Panzer division. They were duly reassured that the din was all our own work. The natives of the main village were anxious too, but not for our safety. They feared for their own lives and homesteads, and we soon found that dumps we had prepared for destruction would be interfered with and the material scattered around. Somewhat naturally, they objected to shells whistling over their thin mud-built walls and to explosions that shook the foundations of dwellings which a heavy rain storm is sufficient to destroy. They were, in any case, unnerved by the evacuation of the British troops and feared reprisals for their formerly helpful attitude towards us at the hands of the enemy who would presumably be following after we had gone. We did what we could to relieve their distress. We made lavish gifts from the remaining food store, feigning generosity and not the compulsion of circumstances which had prevented us from carrying the stuff away. When extra heavy explosions were about to take place, I warned the chief men amongst them, who shepherded the population to their cellars. Nevertheless we were not popular, and it caused concern for a fifth column in our midst, in addition to the anxiety of surprise by the enemy and the problems attending the arrival of G.1 Patrol, for the sake of whose safety we dared not lay protective mines.

The enemy soon took an interest in our lively activities and sent aircraft over regularly, more frequently than they had done during the previous months. After we had blazed away at one of these with small arms fire a two-engined Caproni came down a few miles to the north. I sent a party to deal with it, but it arrived too late; another aircraft landed next to it, and shortly afterwards both flew away. This particular party comprised two trucks with a wireless set under a NCO which had been detached from Group Headquarters and placed under my command to patrol an area north-west of Jalo, and thereby give warning, as far as possible, of enemy approach. After a few days this party was withdrawn after doing excellent work. They had been shot up by enemy aircraft, two of their members being wounded; yet they had still carried on until recalled. They also rescued a number of men of the Rifle Brigade whose truck had stuck when its occupants were trying to escape in an unwise direction and were found by us walking southward. We, in the oasis, saw two unknown trucks one afternoon, presumably a reconnoitring party of the enemy, but they escaped in the heat haze after a chase.

At last we seemed to have destroyed all that it was feasible to disintegrate. Even the wells not required for the use of the villagers were filled with Italian ammunition and jars of sulphuric acid were poured over the contents. Crowbar and burning oil finished off the last of the old Italian Lancias and the last of the bomb dumps, our most difficult subject, had gone up in a pillar of smoke and dust. Twice I had had to re-stock it after partially successful detonations. Each time it meant igniting it with a two-minute fuse, with Wann at the wheel of my P/U fifty yards away, engine running. So now we could move away from the Fort, where we might have been trapped, and take up our watch for G.1 amongst some bushes at Es-Sherif, the extreme north-west corner of the oasis. Here there was good water, whereas the water in the main village was poor, and the natives here were less demoralized, for they willingly brought us eggs and vegetables in exchange for tinned fish and biscuits. From this hiding place we patrolled round the oasis, occasionally returning to the Fort and assuring the natives there that our withdrawal was only temporary and entirely offensive in nature.

Barbour, the signaller, played a fair hand at Bridge; Corporal Stocker knew at least the rudiments of Contract. The difficulty was always to find a fourth. Whenever we got down to initiating a novice something unexpected always happened. On this occasion Guardsman Scourey was making good progress, and we had got to the stage of no longer showing everyone our own hands, when the look out in the crow's nest up a palm-tree called, "Truck Ahoy! On a bearing of 230°, heading north-east". The truck was all alone and was passing rapidly to our south. So, collecting dummy's hand and all dismantled equipment, half of our force of eleven trucks (we had appropriated that which it seemed a pity to destroy) chased off round the edge of the oasis and came up with the solitary truck just after it had reached the Fort. With it were David Stirling, Antony Hunter and Derek Rawnsley, in fact an advance party of the expected Patrol, who had taken the precaution of leaving the other trucks some miles away.

No one of course wanted to stay longer than necessary, and David as usual was in great haste to get back to base and organize a new expedition to destroy the Afrika Korps. G.1 Patrol therefore started off for Siwa that night, and we, after informing Headquarters at Siwa that the Patrols had met and giving the details of G.1's operation previously described, spent a last night on the edge of the oasis and then followed the others home to Siwa.

The Patrol had one more job to do before being sent back to refit in Cairo. 8th Army, which had now consolidated on the Gazala-Bir Hakeim line, after its second hasty withdrawal from the El Agheila-Marada line, urgently required information about the enemy's dispositions and intentions. This was to be achieved by a continuous road watch on all enemy traffic passing along the main roads in the Jebel Akhdar for a period of four days. The task was allotted to "G" Patrol, all that was left of it, under myself.

The only road watch that had taken place before this was one lasting a week in the area near El Agheila, where the country was practically unpopulated, and the road had been observed from a point three miles away. To undertake a similar task in the Jebel presented new problems. The southern road from Barce to Maraua, Slonta and El Faydia, which was likely to be the most heavily used, ran through mountains covered with woods, fields and farmsteads, some European and some native. The northern road, passing near Cyrene, was fifteen miles further north, with large state-subsidised farms between the two roads. The whole area of the hill country of northern Cyrenaica is quite densely populated. To sit in one spot for any length of time is liable to lead to detection.

Selecting the best four trucks of the whole of "G" Patrol and the majority of the remaining members, I organized things on a sound basis of men, equipment and vehicles. To assist us Captain J. E. Haselden, the Mudir of Slonta and Tahib, and a native guide, were attached to us for the operation. It is no over-statement to say that Captain Haselden was the King of the Jebel. He had tramped over it previously in the guise of a native, he spoke Arabic and the dialect of Cyrenaica to perfection, and the natives, who seldom thought highly of white men, would do anything for John Haselden. It is difficult to know what makes a man of one race revered by the members of another. The reason is usually attributed to something magnetic in a man's character, whatever that is. In dealing with the Senussi, whom he knew so well, Haselden had a quiet yet impressive manner. He had a slightly hooked nose and blue eyes full of humour, in the best tradition of a great administrator, and he was an athlete. For me, unacquainted as I was with the local language and customs of thought, the flow of conversation, by which he compelled the members of an unwarlike race to take part in hostilities, was lost in meaning, but I suspect that his ability to maintain such an incessant stream of jokes, ejaculations and gestures of a quality like that of his companions accounted for the regard in which he was held. It was a continual source of amazement to me during this trip to the Jebel how John and his native guides and their countless relations could go on talking and gurgling all day long. But however unintelligible the secret of his power, it certainly worked. I and other Patrol commanders were sometimes let down by native guides if things went wrong, though never betrayed. Yet with Haselden everyone did his bidding with apparent pleasure. Sadly, he was killed when commanding the Commando attack on Tobruk six months later.

Taking with us an extra ration of tea of the green variety popular with Arabs, large tins of dates and a sack of sugar, we set off from Siwa on 9 February. We had weeded out the worst trouble-makers among the trucks, and those we now had behaved excellently. Crossing the Trigh el Abd and passing north through the Stone Belt west of Mekili by a newly dis- covered route, we came to the beginning of the hills.

It was soon quite clear that John Haselden was at home in these parts. A lonely shepherd at the northern end of a large salt lake turned out to be the cousin of one of his best friends. This man led us over some extremely rocky going, little appreciating that we were driving trucks and not camels, into a tiny hollow where a Bedouin camp nestled, the perfection of concealment and camouflage. Here John and I were entertained for at least an hour at the Sheikh's tea party. I sat beside him experiencing my first inoculation of unintelligible chatter, repartee, dramatic stories of grave interest, watching the faces of the gathered tribesmen, some acting as quiet listeners from their positions of relative unimportance by the entrance to the tent, and others near the centre delivering themselves of powerful thoughts, their teeth flashing in the firelight from their dark faces. I kept on nudging John and putting questions to him to ask. Had they seen any enemy near here? If so, how many? What transport? What tanks? Were they patrolling the area to the north of us? After each question I would wait interminably and ask what the answer was. "Oh, we haven't got to that yet," would be the reply, and off they would start talking about what Achmed's uncle had done to the doorkeeper of an Italian colonist. With much handshaking and kissing one's own hand each time one did so, the party finally came to an end. We stopped there that night, drinking bowlsfull of sweet-tasting goat's milk with its ingredient of wild thyme, and moved on north the next morning with another guide who was to contact another, starting a chain of contacts which never seemed to end; for children, brothers and cousins of all contacts were very appreciative of this ambulating sugar and tea canteen, this caravan of Siwa dates.

The information obtained from the local inhabitants was to the effect that an enemy convoy of about two hundred vehicles, comprising guns and tanks, had passed through Cheruba, quite close to the Bedouin camp, two days before. One man who had just come from the hill country reported that the enemy were pushing fairly large forces eastwards along the two main roads, chiefly the southern one. We must therefore reach these and start our watch as soon as possible. On our way further north we stopped to pick up another guide at a concealed well beside the Cheruba-Mekili track, where quantities of semi-derelict British transport had been left behind in the 8th Army's retreat ten days before.

I had a guide sitting on the box behind my head to indicate the way. He was an old man with a particularly raucous voice who kept on shouting "Hek!" and waving his arm. I soon realized that these ejaculations were not intended as an aspersion on my driving but to show me when I should turn to the right or to the left. He probably thought I was too stupid to understand the elements of any real language such as "shemaal" and "yamin", meaning right and left, so it was necessary for my gunner, sitting next to him, to translate his gestures into verbal directives in order to save me from having to observe to my rear as well as to my front. Though aircraft seemed plentiful when we finally stopped, we never noticed them when on the move. The noisy behaviour of our old guide possibly prevented us from heeding such external things.

Further on, when driving up a deep river bed, we came on three natives with a fine chestnut horse. They started to dash off on seeing us, but our native guides ran after them, and they turned out to be close friends of the Mudir of Slonta who was with us. They reported no enemy camps south of the main road. It was considered unwise, however, to drive our trucks to the immediate vicinity of the road and keep them there during our road watch, owing to the large number of natives in this area. By far the majority of them would never dream of disclosing our presence to the enemy, yet in all societies the odd informer exists who will turn traitor, more often to avenge himself on another compatriot, in accordance with the dictates of a family feud, rather than out of enemy sympathies.

Climbing ever higher we finally parked our trucks in the cleft of a small wadi by an upland meadow. Here the Patrol was divided into three parties. The first party under Captain Haselden, with Sergeant Dennis and Guardsmen Matthews, Wilson and Fernback, was to watch the northern of the two main roads. The second party under myself, with six other ranks, would watch the southern road, a distance of about 15 miles by foot to a point on it between Maraua and Slonta, where there was cover close up to its edge. These two parties would carry food for seven days and two blankets per man, for it was very cold at night. They would leave together as soon as possible, and after meeting the first road the first party would continue to a point on the northern road that would be determined by Haselden when the party reached that area. The third party consisted of those remaining behind with the trucks, the drivers and the wireless operator, under the Patrol Sergeant, Sergeant Penfold. Each party would have a native guide to give warning, if occasion should arise, of the approach to our camp of enemy forces, and to act as messengers between each party. The central information bureau, so to speak, where guides would report at intervals, would be the private house of the Mudir of Slonta on the outskirts of that village.

As the march of the first and second parties was fairly long and over difficult country we gladly accepted the offer of the Mudir to provide means of transport for our food and blankets. After waiting several hours one donkey arrived for this purpose. We loaded a few of our blankets on to it, but after a while even this was too much; in fact more effort was spent in putting the donkey on its feet each time it sank down and replacing the load than if we had carried all the kit ourselves. I had left the party with the trucks with some anxiety as the number of natives attracted by our arrival was steadily increasing. Many had news of British soldiers hiding in the hills nearby and making their way back eastward after escaping from the surrounded garrison at Benghazi. Such information provided an excuse for advance payment in dates and tea, and many demanded these commodities for no excuse at all. The aged guide who was left with the third party was the most greedy of these, and for the next week Sergeant Penfold had much difficulty in satisfying his appetite, for he seemed to assume, like his other compatriots, that the whole purpose of our journey was to provide a feast for our well-deserving Libyan allies of the Jebel.

Many aircraft flew overhead all day, and later we ran into a native camp, arousing the usual clamour from the inmates' dogs. We finally reached the southern road at about four in the morning. We rested for two hours and at dawn Haselden's party crossed the road and proceeded towards their objective, the northern road, 15 miles farther.

I and the second party immediately started a look-out post of two men including myself, in a bush a few yards from the road, while the remaining five, including the native guide, hid among some bushes further back. Traffic was not very heavy at first, but at nine o'clock grew much denser, and soon the road was jammed with traffic going east. The vehicles were forced to stop at times, owing to some hold-up further on, and the occupants used to get out of their trucks and walk around until they moved on. We felt after a while unpleasantly close. German soldiers would come and stand about near our bush, and often one felt that their gaze, when directed towards us, could not fail to spot us if this went on much longer. During a period when the traffic was moving again we crept back further from the road, and the one who was observing through field glasses and describing each truck and its contents could now talk in something more than an anxious whisper to the other engaged in writing down the details as fast as he could.

We were too busy watching to our front to be able to observe what was happening on either side. One was only vaguely aware that enemy vehicles were pulling off the road and starting camps; the roaring of their engines as they did so could be heard behind us and to our flank. At lunch time the traffic in the road often stopped and the soldiers would light a fire for their midday meal, and, to provide the wood for it, would cut down branches from bushes which we hoped would not be our own. Early in the afternoon the new relief, another two men of my party, crawled forward and took over from us.

Later, in trying to stalk down to a point near the road from which to take some photographs, I came on some Germans rigging up some tents. On arriving back with the rest of the party, Tahib, our native guide, was found to be in a state of terror. He had been watching my movements and swore that the Germans must have seen me, and probably several of the rest of us as well. The only thing to do, he said, was to pack up and go home. It was difficult to know how much wisdom to attribute to a native guide and I decided that it was best at least to find a slightly different look-out the following day. Even if we had been seen I did not think it likely that the enemy would have taken me for British. He might perhaps send out a party to investigate.

So at dusk the whole party tramped back a mile and lay up for the night in a patch of thick trees. There was some drizzle and sleet and no one got much sleep. Just before dawn the guide and I went off to try to find a more suitable look-out, but ran into another camp, while beyond this, along the road, could be seen a considerable vehicle park. There appeared also to be an enemy shooting party in the neighbourhood behind us. The truth was that this was a very delectable area, at least for those who formed the majority of its inhabitants, nor was it to be wondered at that the commanders of the German units chose this country of streams and woods and fields, where hares and partridges abounded, as good sites for their B Echelon or Rear Divisional Headquarters.

We made our way back to the rest of the party and I started to light a fire in the hope of brewing up a little tea which we all badly needed, but our guide would not countenance the idea. The previous night he had vetoed a fire to warm us on the grounds that it made too much light, and now, in daylight, any smoke would be certain to give us away. At first I thought it wise to observe his advice, but as it became apparent that poor Tahib had really lost his nerve I took little notice of him. One had to humour him to some extent, however, for fear that he would panic and go over to the enemy. That evening a much better guide joined us, reporting that Haselden's party was safely in position on the northern road. His name was Abdul Chadi and he had run into one of the new German camps. There he had been questioned by a German officer, but had been allowed to go, and joined us. I went out that night with Tahib and found a place for a look-out which we moved to before dawn, and from here we continued our watch for the next three days and nights. Owing to the difficulty of moving about unseen in daylight, each pair doing road watch would remain at their post, about two hundred yards from the road, for twelve hours, between dawn and dusk, dusk and dawn. It rained a good deal and snowed at times. When on watch one had to keep very still and one used to long for the twelfth hour when one could get back to the bush that was our headquarters and get something hot to drink. By this time I had insisted on a fire for a short time.

At the end of the first day I had sent Corporal Stocker back on foot to report the summary of the road traffic for transmission by wireless to Siwa. So we now consisted of Corporal Hird, Corporal Fraser, Waiting, Allen, Gibson, who, though a driver, had volunteered to do the road watch, and myself. After a few days our more palatable rations had been consumed, for the two guides, who had no food with them, had disposed of our tea and tinned fish and fruit, but by the fourth day they were obliged to be less fastidious and share our bully beef, which was all we had left. Our emergency rations were eked out, small pieces being broken off and dissolved in hot water as a sort of cocoa. Our guides also had insufficient clothing to give them warmth and we had to provide one of our blankets for each of them at night. In spite of their disadvantages, however, our Senussi friends were quite useful, particularly Abdul Chadi. They used to fill our water bottles from nearby pools of rain water and make reconnaissance patrols, for it mattered little if they were seen by the enemy.

On the fourth night I sent them out to the point where Haselden's party had crossed our road to warn them on their return of the newly formed enemy encampments. But they returned at dawn not having contacted Haselden. This made me somewhat anxious, for I had had no word from him since the second day. He might have come through that night without the guides seeing him, or he might have well been spotted by the enemy and be in a hurry to get away once he reached the trucks. Alternatively, he might have been caught, or again, he might not have come south at all yet. In any case he was due back not later than the next night. In the afternoon of the fifth day from the start of the road watch we started back for the trucks and arrived there to our relief that night.

I had left Sergeant Penfold with detailed written orders covering all possible contingencies: his action in the event of either of the road watch parties not returning, or of the enemy discovering his own position. However, we found all was well. The only drawback was that too many people were sharing in our prosperity. The number of cousins of our native assistants had increased out of all proportion and all showed evident disappointment on discovering that our fund of dates and goodies was not inexhaustible.

Yet we had other very welcome guests. Two officers of the Welch Regiment, Major Gibson and Captain Hammond, had been picked up and brought to us by natives after various adventures in their escape from Benghazi. Three British soldiers had also turned up. Among the non-Europeans who had booked tickets to Siwa there were: twelve soldiers of the Libyan Arab Force and one "recruit" who aspired to join the same unit; one native who might be termed refugee, having done in several Italian colonists and wanting to leave the district; a number of guides, and our friend the Mudir of Slonta, who had decided that it was no longer safe for him and his family in their homeland and warned us that he wanted accommodation for his son, two wives and some other belongings. Sergeant Penfold had also received a note from a British officer, Lieutenant Dodds, RA, who was lying wounded in a native camp some fifty miles to the south. He had evidently heard that a British unit was in the neighbourhood, but, being ignorant of the military situation, had send us a note stating, "Am wounded. Please send ambulance for evacuation to CCS".

On my arrival we distributed the remainder of our special stores to all the Libyans. In spite of the worries they had caused Sergeant Penfold, they had proved useful in telling tall stories as to our identity to those passing shepherds who, they considered, should not be "in the know". We lay down to sleep and soon John Haselden and his party arrived. They had completed the thirty-mile return journey from the northern road in fourteen hours carrying considerable equipment. The road had been watched for nearly four days from the top of a cliff overlooking it as it descends into a ravine. A log of all the vehicles that passed confirmed that the road, though considerably used, was not as popular as the southern one. On one occasion John had borrowed the clothing of a passing shepherd, had dressed himself in it, and had led a slightly suspicious herd of goats to the verge of the road in order better to observe some details of the markings on the enemy trucks.

That night is very clear in my memory. I lay in my warm sleeping bag at last. Everything was quiet in our wadi-valley, the stars shining above the black hillsides. Then every half hour or so a coyote, or wild dog, would howl into the night and a chorus of howls would follow until soon everything was quiet again. It was a weird form of disassociation with our war and its exertions.

We hoped to move off early next morning, but there was some delay. The Mudir's family arrived at last with an assortment of baggage including goats and chickens. The normal capacity of our 30-cwt trucks was three or four men including the driver, in addition to our operational equipment and stores. Now we set off with our four trucks carrying no less than forty-seven human beings with both normal and much more abnormal baggage. It is well known that the Arab does not consider a vehicle properly used until every appendage and cubic inch of space has been utilized. In this respect we had truly gone native. A basket or bundle swung from each gun mounting, cooking utensils dangled from channel irons and the cackle and bleating of livestock vied with the chatter of their owners in drowning the drone of our engines.

The heavy rains, though they had not much affected our trucks in their camping place high up on the hills, had filled the lower valleys and the plain to the south with flood water. We had some difficulty crossing the flood, which covered the Mekili-Cheruba track, and prayed that no aircraft would come to attack so concentrated a target. One great advantage of the rain, however, was that we could travel fast without throwing up dust. We travelled south all day, picking up Lieutenant Dodds at his native camp, passed through the Thermos Bomb area at dusk and halted that night in the safe ground south of Trigh el Abd.

We reached Siwa at lunchtime two days later. Here we were given orders to go on at once to Cairo to refit. We were relieved of the majority of our guests, but kept the British soldiers and officers, as well as the Mudir and his family, all of whom we had to take to Cairo. A critical problem arose at Matruh as to where we could park them for the night while the rest of us enjoyed the bar and canteen of the military transit camp, a kind

1. The Author (*right*) with Corporal (later Sergeant) Malcolm Fraser.

2. The Author on the Fayoum Lake, Summer 1942. Note the bandaged desert sores.

3. David Stirling leaning against the wireless truck.

4. Captain Dick Lawson, LRDG Medical Officer.

5. Guy Prendergast (*right*) with Jake Easonsmith, respectively C.O. and 2 i/c of LRDG (*IWM HU25156*).

6. *Left to right*: Tim Heywood, Plugs Ashdown, Bill Kennedy Shaw, Guy Prendergast.

7. *Left to right:* David Lloyd Owen, Jake Easonsmith, Gus Holliman.

8. *Left to right:* Anthony Hunter, Ken Lazarus, Dick Croucher, Tony Hay, the Author, Jake Easonsmith (*IWM HU25251*)

9. Guardsman Thomas Wann, the Author's soldier servant; note the Guards pennant (*see p.41*).

10. John Haselden dressed as a Bedouin (*see p.64*). Behind him is a Ford truck (*IWM HU16530*).

11. "The LRDG possessed two aircraft of its own..." (*p. 23*). Guy Prendergast with the WACO which he flew himself (*IWM HU24959*).

12. G.1. Patrol, Siwa, December 1941. Standing on the rear truck is Sergeant Dennis (*see p. 67*) (*IWM HU16614*).

13. Robin Gurdon (*right*) with Lord Gilford in December 1941, before Robin joined the LRDG.

of Mecca for members of Western Desert Force, now 8th Army, where you met scores of friends you had not seen since school-days. In accordance with John Haselden's instructions we had to dump the Mudir at a camp outside the town which appeared to be reserved for native prisoners. I told the Commandant all I could in the Mudir's favour, but nothing reassured the old boy that the barbed wire and sentries represented the proper abode for an honoured guest. He looked much relieved next morning when we picked him up with his family. We finally delivered him the following day to Major Anderson of the Organization for Enemy Occupied Territory (OETA) in Cairo.

Our trucks by this time were running on more oil than petrol and three out of the six were being towed. We halted in front of Mena House Hotel, below the Great Pyramid of Giza, to fill them up with a last dose of oil before smoking our way into Cairo. Here we also conducted the rustic ritual of our midday brew up among the civilized amenities of Giza. The most remarkable instance of divination occurred at the Midan Ismailia at the entrance to Cairo, where we paused to reassemble in the traffic. Major Peter de Salis was walking by, smartly dressed as a Coldstream officer in service dress. He went up to the man with the longest beard among us and instantly said, "Well, Scourey, how are you?" Having become accustomed to seeing Scourey in this condition, I personally did not recognize him the next day, at Abbassia, when the reverse process had taken place.

After disposing of our equipment and trucks at the LRDG store-rooms and the workshops at Abbassia, the Patrol was sent off on ten days' leave, the Coldstreamers making for their haunts in Alexandria, where they had been stationed before the war, and the Scots Guardsmen for the familiar scenes of Cairo. I myself spent a night and day of hot baths, cold drinks, good food and gaberdine comfort and then drove off with Wann (my soldier servant) to visit the two Battalions, then at Cheruba on the Gazala line (west of Tobruk) about five hundred and fifty miles mostly by road. Besides wishing to see old friends again, it was urgent to obtain reinforcements to replace those we had lost, or who had become ill, or who needed a change. I also looked forward to a new Coldstream officer, a counterpart to myself. This was, by my good fortune, Robin Gurdon, about whom I shall now write at some length.

When Robin and I settled down at base at Siwa, one of our first tasks was to decide which of the thirty-eight or so men should be in his half patrol G.2, or mine G.1. We had to get the balance fair and equal. Robin should have Corporal Stocker as chief navigator since he, a newcomer, must have the most experienced navigator. I was desperate to have Scott as my fitter, mainly because of his phenomenal eyesight, though his skill as a fitter was just as significant. Robin's jobs turned out largely to take parties of the SAS, usually David Stirling himself, to aerodromes, and such parties were pretty reckless in their treatment of enemy aircraft (even when in the air). The less Robin saw of them the better for his peace of mind. A difficult choice arose over one non-commissioned officer who was apt to play the tough guy. Though a good man at heart, he annoyed me. "You had better let me handle Corporal X" Robin said. I was thankful for this solution. Robin's manner of authority and humour was of the kind that made anyone do what he wanted and this difficult character would have been happy to support anything he ordered.

It is in bad taste to subject excellent men to eulogy especially if you get to know them well. It is best to keep to the effect that such people have on others. I describe later the incident when a colonel stood to attention in his own office and called Robin "Sir", though Robin was a subaltern. Robin did not even notice. The situation seemed entirely natural to him.

In fact practically all situations were natural to him, though he injected a good deal of his own preferences into what he did and whom he did it with. He hated the war, but he was determined to take an active and effective part in trying to win it. When most of his contemporaries, 38 years old or more, were seeking ways of making warfare not too dangerous or arduous, he had different ideas. Like his father who had fought with distinction in the first war and had to neglect for a long time his farm in Kenya, Robin surrendered his directorships in the City and of Imperial Airways and became a platoon commander in the desert. When he could have accompanied Oliver Lyttelton to Washington with the rank of Lieutenant Colonel and taken part in similar missions, he volunteered to join the LRDG.

The nearest we got to the comforts of peacetime luxury at Siwa was bathing in a remote pool among palm trees called "the Sheikh's Pool". The water was absolutely clear, being well away from donkeys, goats, sheep and their owners. Bubbles came up to the surface continuously from some piping at the bottom. I could not reach it as it was too deep for my ears to take the water pressure, so I could never discover its origin – whether modern or Roman, as some of the large marble pools were, or even Alexandrine. What mattered most to us was the way our pieces of Lanvin or Bourgeois soap were getting smaller. With their disintegration, civilization really was in a bad way.

"You rather like beat-ups," Robin once said to me as we sat in our canvas camp chairs in our sitting room one evening back at base. We had a small concrete house to ourselves and soldier servants. Robin's bedroom and mine, with our camp beds, were on either side of the sitting room. By this remark he meant that I was more bloodthirsty than he, and that he preferred reconnaissance and taxi-parties – taking other people to their destinations. I admitted that the more destruction one could do the better the odds of getting the war over, but I did not *enjoy* the whole thing any more than he did. I also longed to get back to the England we knew, especially the rural life.

One of our worries was the way too many people back in England were planning a different kind of country to the one we loved. *Picture Post* would present a smug solution to all our social anomalies – typical of a socialist authoritarian state which Herbert Morrison and some members of the War Cabinet were increasingly advocating. Quite the opposite was illustrated by American weekly and monthly publications such as the *Saturday Evening Post*, copies of which were sent to Robin by his wife Yoskyl who was in America. There the attitude of those who produced popular illustrated magazines was: "We will decide on what happens in our country, politically and socially, when our boys come home from the War. They must be there to decide on what sort of life we are going to live. They are fighting for the country they know and love. They must be at the front of things in peace as they are now in war." These things worried Robin and me. They worried me even more when I got back in a hospital ship in February 1944 to find so many people complaining how little we were doing to help the Russians.

I have often considered how Robin would have taken such changes as we have had since 1945, had he survived. He represented all that was best in the English way of life, with its fairness, good manners and good humour. His Patrol thought the world of him and when they disobeyed his last command they could scarcely do otherwise, as described later. Although he had two 20mm cannon shells and one 8mm bullet in his lungs and stomach he told his Patrol to continue with the operation and raid the Fuka aerodrome, the second of David Stirling's orders. He had already completed the first on the night before. There are not many people with such high standards.

Chapter Five

THE LULL BEFORE
THE STORM

In March 1942 8th Army and Rommel faced each other on the Gazala Line. Both had offensive ambitions, largely dependent on the scales of supply which they respectively enjoyed.

Battle was to erupt at the end of May, and it was to lead to the loss of Tobruk, its garrison, and the mass of stores accumulated there with a view to sustaining 8th Army's renewed advance westwards; and to the retreat of 8th Army to the Alamein position where the final confrontation with Rommel would take place.

During this period before the battle the LRDG was under direct command of 8th Army, and was required to carry out contradictory tasks – the observation of traffic on the enemy's roads, and the disruption of that traffic. The former task (recognized as being the more important) was carried out more successfully than the latter.

After their ten days' leave the members of the Patrol re-assembled at Abbassia to proceed with the business of re-equipment. Some members, it is true, had to return to barracks after only two days' leave, finding that the financial remuneration of a soldier did not meet the expenses of the recreation he deserved. A number of new members joined us from both Battalions. Each of these was interviewed by Robin Gurdon and myself, and we were pleased with the way the Battalions had sent us some of their best material. Our poor old Fords had been dumped at Tel el Kebir and turned out to a paddock for the rest of their lives, so we expected, but wrongly, for in their old age some months later they were put into harness and ridden west again.

Our new chargers were impressive. They were 30-cwt Chevrolet trucks specially fitted out for us. They featured streamlined bonnets, silent engines and low petrol consumption, but one important disadvantage: they had no four-wheel drive. They were equipped with what was commonly called a "booster" gear, which, as purists insisted on explaining, merely provided an auxiliary gearbox ratio.

Considerable latitude was given to Patrol commanders in the manner in which they had their machine guns mounted, in the number of guns carried and in methods of camouflaging their equipment. In the last respect "G" Patrol adopted an original colour scheme. We took each of them off in turn to a helpful paint shop where it was sprayed the most glorious pink, yellow and green. If they did not elude detection from enemy aircraft they would at least dazzle them. When first sprayed, they did look a little flashy. Corporal Inwood, the first driver to take one over, said he would not be seen in Cairo driving such a thing, but discipline overcame embarrassment. I must say there was no doubt that one could see a "G" Patrol truck a mile away even in the thick traffic of Sharia Ibrahim Pasha and this did not auger well for concealment in an open featureless plain. I assured my troops that the colours would soon tone down and that the trucks would become as good as chameleons eventually.

By now Lewis guns had gone right out of fashion. We liked something with more punch and fire power. A number of .303 Brownings, some Vickers gas-operated machine guns, as well as an odd Spandau, Bren and Breda had been acquired. We also had, in accordance with establishment, water-cooled Vickers guns both .303" and 0.5". For a larger calibre gun the 37mm Bofors had been scrapped and the 20mm Breda introduced instead. Each half-Patrol had six Chevrolet trucks and in one of these was mounted this Breda gun for dealing with major targets both in the air and on the ground. Navigational kit – theodolites, sun compasses, azimuth cards, navigation books, chronometers – were overhauled and deficiencies were replaced. In addition to our two navigators, Corporal Stocker and Guardsman Leach, it was decided to train two more guardsmen, namely Crossley and Blaney, so that each half-Patrol would have a chief and second navigator.

Every morning at 8.45 Robin would arrive outside my flat with his car and chauffeur from David Wills' flat on Gezira Island, hoot the horn three times to signal his invariably punctual arrival, and off we would go to supervise the distribution of our new kit at Abbassia requiring adaptations and re-adjustments, and also to do what training we could. Little progress could be made in this respect, except in firing our various weapons on a classification range. We would wait until we got to Siwa for more realistic forms of training.

One day in Cairo Robin asked Peter Fleming to lunch with us in the garden restaurant at Shepheard's. I did not know him but Robin of course did. He had just flown out from England the night before, over-flying the Continent and the Mediterranean in a Liberator at maximum height, as was the usual practice. He was dressed as a major in the Grenadiers and wearing service dress uniform. Peter Fleming was then regarded as one of the Allies' experts on Russia. I suppose that his book *News from Tartary*, on his journey with Kini Maillart across Siberia, must have had something to do with this reputation. Anyway, here he was, having just come from Russia a month ago, with the 1942 campaign about to begin. "It was a miracle," he said, "that the Russians weren't defeated last year. There isn't a hope that they will survive this year. And then what friends and allies have we got left?" The Japanese had sunk the battleship *Prince of Wales* and battle cruiser *Repulse* a few months earlier off the coast of Malaya. They were now in Papua New Guinea and getting closer to Australia. The American and Australian Navies were doing all they could under Admiral Nimitz, but we had very few land forces to stop the Japanese from taking Burma and entering India. There was practically nothing in Syria and Palestine if the Germans invaded the Middle East over the Caucasus. The so-called 9th Army near Damascus and Beirut was an army only on paper. Peter was on his way to contact the Chinese, practically the only allies we had left, to fight on land. Then he would go on to see what were the odds on landings in Australia.

It certainly was a memorable meeting, this lunch at Shepheard's in March 1942. The background was a nadir of the war and went on until the Germans stopped on the Alamein Line early in July and were repulsed at Alam Halfa at the end of August. Yet most of us never accepted the possibility of defeat.

Siwa required our presence as soon as possible, but before we finally left on 22 March we bought a considerable quantity of NAAFI goods. We found by experience that our Heavy Section was unable to bring up the amenities of life such as cigarettes, tinned fruit, tinned milk, chocolate and beer, except at very infrequent intervals. Robin and I therefore bought a fair stock of these, as a private canteen for the Patrol, though not much beer could be carried. We naturally also bought for ourselves a reasonable stock of whisky, various tinned foods and fruit (but Robin did not like pineapple), a great deal of Nescafe and the self-operating variety of soda water syphon, together with innumerable sparklets of compressed air which still rattle about like moth balls in the bottom of my luggage today. Michael Crichton Stuart came to visit us the day before we left and presented a gift of additional goodies for the Patrol. Even if these luxuries would not see us through the coming summer, they would help us to re-acclimatize ourselves to life further west.

In addition to the twelve 30-cwts we had one 15-cwt P/U for the whole Patrol in which Robin Gurdon and I led our little convoy down the road from Cairo to Amiriya, then along the coast road to Mersa Matruh, where we turned off south-west along the track to Siwa, a journey of about five hundred miles, taking two days without hurrying.

The way to Siwa turns left off the main coast road at Mersa Matruh. Shortly after leaving Matruh we had been told to stop at a REME depot where we were to collect some jerricans, a new form of petrol container. They were the very first batch that had been collected from the Germans and the LRDG was the first and only unit to be issued with them. We were shown into the Commandant's office, where the colonel was sitting at his desk. Robin walked in slightly ahead of me. We were both wearing our Hebron sheepskin coats and service dress caps, his with Coldstream badge and mine Scots Guards. The REME colonel rose to his feet and addressing Robin asked, "What can I do for you, Sir?" Robin's two stars were under his coat and my three obviously did not show. We explained our mission which they had expected. We loaded up with the jerricans and drove off. I said to Robin later, "It was amusing when he called you 'Sir'." "Oh! Did he?" said Robin, "I didn't notice."

For a few days at Siwa we started various types of training. It consisted chiefly of practising what we would do in all the imagined situations that might arise when on an operation. Each truck in turn tried firing at different types of targets when on the move. On the edge of the sand sea, bordering the oasis, a course with a three-mile circuit was laid out. As each truck came over a dune or around a corner, it would be confronted with a tar barrel ahead or a stack of old petrol cans to the flank. Points were given to each gunner according to his skill in firing at the targets. I introduced other more complicated tactics, such as dismounted action, and here a machine gun from each truck had to be dismounted and carried to a firing position. If attacked by more than one aircraft at a time it was highly dangerous to remain by one's vehicle. A twin-engine ME110 with two 20mm cannon and several 8mm machine guns, light-armour-protected, was more than a match for several of our 30-cwts. We tried out open formation when on the move, so as to bring maximum firepower on the enemy and not on ourselves. The crew of the 20mm Breda was trained in getting into action quickly. A kite was made and towed behind the P/U travelling in a large ellipse to provide a target simulating an aircraft. Captured contraceptives from the Italian army were made into balloons for the same purpose. Not having any hydrogen, we tried launching them from the top of an escarpment, but they obstinately made straight for the ground and burst there. They couldn't have been much good for their intended purpose.

Robin's half of the Patrol was now called G.2 and mine G.1. As Tony Hay, with the rank of Captain, had been captured the previous December, I was moved up a rank and my half-Patrol became G.1. Robin, being a newcomer, had the rank of Lieutenant. This did not necessarily mean any interchange in the members of the Patrols.

Only a few days after our arrival at Siwa both G.1 and G.2 were called out on operations.

At the beginning of March 1942 a Patrol of the LRDG began a continuous road watch on the main road not far from El Agheila. This road watch was maintained for four months without a break, Patrols relieving one another in turn, and each one carrying out the watch for a period of about ten days. Information gained by this means was sent back by wireless as each Patrol left the area of the look-out, but important information was sent back immediately, such as when 107 tanks passed east on 14 March. On 30 March G.2 Patrol left Siwa to take part in this census of enemy traffic. GHQ Middle East set much store by the information obtained by this method. Our submarines of the Royal Navy prevented the enemy from using the harbours of Cyrenaica to the extent he wished and he was compelled to unload much of his supplies at Tripoli, a safer distance from our naval bases in the eastern Mediterranean. By keeping a record, transmitted by wireless, of all supplies passing near El Agheila an accurate estimate was obtained of all reinforcements and fresh supplies which the enemy's main forces received by way of Tripoli.

In order to obtain the best results GHQ had issued to us a detailed questionnaire relating to the types of enemy troops, equipment, stores and vehicle markings we were likely to see. The also sent an intelligence officer, Captain Enoch Powell, to explain this questionnaire to members of our Patrols. "Grey matter", as he was called on account of his evident learning and his past experience as a University Professor, brought with him also an album of photographs of all the latest types of enemy equipment. Before going to carry out a road watch every man was made familiar with these photographs and Captain Powell used to impress on everyone the subtle differences between the chassis and turrets on different tanks, the recuperators of guns and the exact position of a tap on a petrol or water trailer. It was not possible to take these excellent pictures on operations, but lots of notes and some pamphlets were kept by Patrols and issued to each pair as they took their turn at the look-out.

The members of G.2 Patrol absorbed all this detailed information with due regard for its importance. Some of this information, we hoped, would not only keep the command of 8th Army informed as to what it had to contend with, but would brief GHQ and Naval Intelligence about which enemy convoys had got through.

As Jalo was now occupied by the enemy the Patrol made a detour around the southern side of this oasis in order to avoid possible detection in crossing the tracks between Jalo and the coast. It also reduced the risk of encountering enemy aircraft looking out for the SAS and ourselves in that area. On this occasion the Patrol covered 221 miles in one day without travelling before sunrise or after sunset, a figure never exceeded at that time of the year in the desert. Some very bad going was met with before crossing the Marada-El Agheila road at dusk on the following day. The next day the Patrol contacted the guide of T.2 Patrol at the appointed rendezvous. That evening they took over the road watch from the New Zealanders as well as the hidden site of their encampment.

The observation post where each pair in turn carried out their traffic census was not normally fixed at any definite spot. At a certain point about 300 yards from the road a pit had been dug and a cover placed over it, sprinkled with sand and stones, so that only a small aperture remained through which those inside could peer at the road in front of them. This was used for a considerable time by various Patrols, but some preferred to hide up in a position less compromising if they were spotted. In spite of the extreme flatness and lack of cover, it was possible to find here and there a tiny patch of scrub within three or four hundred yards of the road's edge. It was only possible, of course, for reliefs to take over the watch during the hours of dusk or darkness.

Interference by the enemy, or from other outside sources, at times caused some anxiety, but did not lead to the suspension of the road watch during this whole period of four months. The most usual cause of anxiety was the occasional passage of Bedouin with their flocks of goats and camels. The natives of Tripolitania were much less friendly than those of Cyrenaica; in fact they were actually hostile further west. They would usually recognize us as British. Later on this summer when one of the New Zealand Patrols was on watch some Bedouin even resorted to blackmail, requiring bribes in food and cash for their silence. One of them went up to a German officer standing near the look-out post and pointed out to him the spot where the two observers lay. These soon stood up and walked slowly off while the German officer took no action. But such trouble from the Bedouin was unusual and none occurred on this occasion with G.2 Patrol. For two days a party of natives and their camels stayed in the area and showed some curiosity in the Patrol, but took no disturbing action. Nor did the Germans, as happened on occasions later, show signs of suspicion and search the area with a dog; neither did they pitch a temporary camp in the neighbourhood, as they sometimes did.

Robin Gurdon's report is very comprehensive and gives much information which was valuable at that time, but has little interest now. The only detail worth recording is that he reports

"The enemy M/T was on the whole in distinctly good order. There was a considerable proportion of completely new vehicles, and moribund lorries were not plentiful." This observation shows the very different state of affairs regarding the condition of enemy transport noted a month earlier by John Haselden and me in the Jebel of Cyrenaica.

On its return trip the Patrol passed north of Jalo, crossing a number of fresh tracks. Late one afternoon they were spotted by an Italian reconnaissance aircraft. It circled round them several times, but flew off without attacking. The Patrol moved off thirty miles before camping for the night. It reached Siwa without further incident on 17 April.

Meanwhile G.1 Patrol and I had completed a short operation near Jalo, connected with plans in the air, encouraged, if not conceived, by John Haselden (now a Lieutenant-Colonel on the staff of 8th Army HQ) for making a raid on Jalo. I was all for it. We now had the advantage of knowing the geography of the place accurately. My "scorched palm" action in January had not made it unserviceable for a new enemy garrison. Haselden put forward plans for an operation involving three LRDG Patrols which were to seize the fort, the officers' mess and the school (used as barracks), kill or capture the whole garrison, destroy their stores and their aircraft and then probably vacate the oasis. On account of its size, Jalo required a large garrison to provide an adequate defence, and it would be unwise to try to retain it for long. These attractive speculations, however, never materialized, though some preparation was made by an effort to discover as much as possible of the enemy's dispositions and strength in Jalo through the medium of two Senussi spies. It was the initial task of G.1 Patrol to take them there.

On the way we passed Jarabub, so that the two Senussi might say their prayers at the famous mosque, and to enable us to collect wood for our fires and brew-ups. The storage of fuel for fires was now a problem. Originally our petrol tins were provided in expendable wooden cases which did not prevent the tins from leaking, but made excellent fuel, being well seasoned with petrol. These had later been replaced by some miserable carton cases, which did even less to prevent the petrol cans from leaking, but afforded us no compensating advantage. Recently we had been equipped on the jerrican basis. All other units had reluctantly been compelled to give up the jerricans they captured from the enemy, and they had been allocated to the exclusive use of the LRDG. Jerricans were excellent in every way except that they were too good at their job. There was nothing expendable about them. Not only did they have no wooden containers, but we were not allowed to discard them when empty and had to forgo the pleasure of seeing our truck-loads diminish in capacity during the course of an operation. Those who travelled on the back of a truck were encumbered by the bulkiest part of our freight from the beginning of the operation to the end. In the valleys around Jarabub, however, were to be found the remains of disused store depots and camp sites of former garrisons, and here we would often stop on the way out to an operation and stack our trucks with sufficient fire-wood for the journey. Hence the popularity of Jarabub, in other respect unsalubrious, putrid with flies and mosquito-ridden in its limestone depression. The sacred shrine and mosque, so important to the Senussi, were beyond our level of culture at that time.

We reached Chetmir, a point fifteen miles from Jalo on the edge of the sand sea, on the evening of the following day. From here, with two trucks, I drove up close to the edge of the oasis at night and dropped our two Senussi companions. They were due to report back two days later at a large hump near Chetmir, which I had previously pointed out to them. Early the next morning we shifted our camp a short distance away to a point where we could observe the rendezvous and anyone approaching it. This was a precaution against the spies being caught and questioned by the enemy and disclosing our position. We would also not be taken by surprise if the spies, on returning, were followed by an enemy party.

Nothing eventful happened during our wait. Some aircraft were heard now and then but not seen. We were also visited by a wandering Senussi native from a small oasis, Jekerra, to the north of Jalo. He was engaged in trapping small desert rats, two of which he showed us, his hands trembling with fright – from us, not the real desert rats. There was a considerable number of both Italians and Germans, he said, at Jalo but none at Aujila or in his own small oasis. The natives were, apparently, very poor and had almost nothing to eat, for the enemy did little to improve their condition, and they much regretted the departure of the British. After making him swear by Allah not to say a word of our presence and giving him a little tea and sugar, I let him go, in case his relatives sent out a search party, and I told him to call the next day, when he would be given more food. On the next day the two Senussi spies we had deposited returned on foot from Jalo with much valuable information, a summary of which I sent in a signal to Headquarters that evening. Late in the day the solitary native duly returned from Jekerra. I gave him a good deal of sugar and tea, and then we started for home, reaching Siwa on 5 April in under a day and a half. The route was the usual one, known as the Gareba track, running east and west along the northern edge of the Great Sand Sea.

This too was fast travelling and, as with G.2 Patrol, our new Chevrolet trucks were proving fast and reliable. Their engines hardly ever gave trouble. Yet they had two serious disadvantages. The first, that of having no four-wheel drive, has already been referred to, and this rendered every journey through soft sand or over mud flats arduous. Secondly, they were so constructed that the centre of gravity was very near the rear axle, with the result that numerous blow-outs occurred with the tyres on the rear wheels whenever the trucks were overloaded. At the start of an operation they invariably were overloaded. But these disadvantages were not experienced in the first two trips after our refit in Cairo. Later, in the heat of the summer; things were different. Tyre pressure became a serious problem. There followed now a considerable pause between operations as far as the two "G" Patrols were concerned.

In addition to the training described in the previous chapter I also tried to introduce some intellectual exercise. We would have a debate. The subject to be debated would be non-political, but I hoped it would stimulate the minds of all members of my Patrol and lead to some unexpected thinking. The men chose the subject "History is bunk", a remark attributed to Henry Ford. Corporal Stocker, the only non-guardsman and my chief navigator (before Corporal Leach), volunteered to oppose the motion. Sergeant Dennis was the proposer. Two others volunteered as seconders. I acted as Speaker, which meant more-or-less, non-speaking. Stocker manfully tried to roll back the prevailing "ignorance is bliss", but with little support. "If you know nothing of the past," Sergeant Dennis would argue, "then you would have no grudge against anyone. Wars are caused by someone seeking revenge." The "Ayes" had it. Best not to know too much. Perhaps Sergeant Dennis and Henry Ford were right. We had left our Ford trucks at Abbassia a month earlier and had exchanged them ungratefully for Chevrolets; but we would later, that coming Autumn, need them back again. If the statement attributed to him is true, Henry Ford's openness of mind stood us in good stead. I wished we had one of the pre-war explorers with us at the time, such as our own Commanding Officer, Guy Prendergast, to remind us of the excellent Model T Fords which they used in search of the lost oasis, Zerzura.

For over a month I, with G.1, remained at Siwa training and preparing for the attack on Jalo and other targets, but these operations were cancelled before inception. G.2 spent a fortnight at Siwa between their road-watch and their series of three operations in the Benghazi area. The first two of these are described next.

On 2 May G.2 set forth from Siwa for the area north of Msus and east of Benghazi. They were to transport a party under Captain Bob Melot, of G (R) Department Middle East Headquarters, an officer of the ISLD, and two Arabs, who were all being sent out for purposes of reconnaissance close to the enemy's main centres. Travelling very fast Gurdon reached the area of his destination in two days, a distance of 430 miles. He passed close by Msus at night. The passengers were duly dropped and met various agents whom they were to contact in the district. Nothing eventful occurred except that the Patrol could watch from quite close the RAF bombing Benghazi during the night. Not wasting any time on their return, 400 miles were completed in two days. It was observed that the inland tracks between Msus and Mekili were extensively used by the enemy. No enemy aircraft interfered throughout the trip, and finally Siwa was reached six days after leaving it.

G.2 left again on its next operation a week later. Its new job entailed taking Major David Stirling with Lieutenants Fitzroy Maclean, Randolph Churchill, Gordon Alston, Ken Allott, Corporal Seekings, Corporal Cooper (David Stirling's famous accomplice and bodyguard) and other members of the SAS with David's "Blitzwagon" to blow up the shipping in Benghazi harbour.

Apart from G.2 Patrol, the party had the help of S.2 Rhodesian Patrol under John Olivey to guide, reconnoitre and transport what turned out to be a complicated operation. A party of the Special Boating Section, a successor to Bob Laycock's commando, accompanied Stirling's SAS parties. The SBS under Ken Allott and David Sutherland had a captured German staff car, but it was badly damaged on the way out by a thermos bomb near Trigh-el-Abd, which wounded Sutherland, so that he had to return to Siwa with a section of the two LRDG Patrols. Captain Bob Melot also took part for his expertise in language and knowledge of the country. Finally, Paddy Mayne was included with a party of SAS to concentrate on aircraft and storage plant destruction. After taking the SAS close to Benghazi, G.2 Patrol was to destroy the railway line to Barce while waiting for Stirling and others to return.

The outward trip was made in good time. Before the SAS drove into Benghazi, the whole party laid up for a day in the comparatively densely populated district south of Benina. Numerous natives were met, and two lost members of the Libyan Arab Force were picked up. Aircraft of all kinds, mostly enemy, were numerous. At dusk on the fourth day after leaving Siwa Stirling's party drove on to the main road and bluffed their way through the town's defences without being challenged. This is not the occasion to attempt an adequate description of a highly colourful incident in the operations of the SAS. Though the attempt to destroy shipping in Benghazi harbour failed, it was not through lack of daring, for never in the course of the war was there any parallel with this visit by a British force, dressed in British uniforms, spending two nights on the quayside of an enemy-held capital city and the day in one of its houses. G.2 Patrol were glad to be associated with this performance.

During the first night, meanwhile, the Patrol set explosive charges on the railway lines, but these were apparently discovered, for a train passed by two days later without causing an explosion.

Stirling's parties duly returned from their escapades and the Patrol set off for Siwa, reaching it without incident three days later on 26 May, one day before the enemy attacked the 8th Army on the Gazala line.

Before continuing with the LRDG's activities during the battles of Gazala and Knightsbridge, it is necessary to return to the beginning of May to record G.2 Patrol's next operation.

At this time 8th Army, on the Gazala line, issued instructions to the LRDG which in practice were difficult to co-ordinate. "It is estimated," states an 8th Army Operation Instruction, "that more than half of the enemy's maintenance tonnage for Cyrenaica is going by road from Tripoli to Benghazi, and our policy from now until further orders will be to interrupt this road movement." The Instruction continues: "Information about enemy road movements from Tripolitania to Cyrenaica and between eastern and western Cyrenaica is of vital importance, and the obtaining of it must on no account be jeopardized by other operations."

The LRDG was thus required to provide information about enemy road movements both west of Cyrenaica and inside Cyrenaica itself. This task had first priority. And, secondly, enemy communications west of El Agheila were to be interrupted by offensive action. As has been pointed out before, these two types of operation are difficult to reconcile.

The role of primary importance was already being carried out, as we have seen, by a continuous road-watch at Marble Arch west of El Agheila. A second continuous watch was later established covering the inland tracks west of Mekili. In addition, the main roads in northern Cyrenaica were kept under observation by parties provided by G (R), and in particular by a small force of British officers and mostly native other ranks under Major Peniakoff (Popski). Such parties as these came under the control of the LRDG when in the field, and we were largely responsible for their supplies and their communications. We used to deliver recharged electric batteries and millions of lire in cash to a man on a camel who was part of Popski's mafia. Thus we now had to consider how to carry out an offensive policy without adversely affecting this system of reconnaissance.

G.1 (my Patrol) and T.2 (Nick Wilder's New Zealand Patrol) were given orders to carry out raids without so arousing enemy retaliation as to endanger the road-watch parties. Attempts were made to devise a method of destroying enemy vehicles without the enemy finding out how the destruction was done, or at least the areas where the aggressors operated. It was hoped at first to give the enemy the impression that the losses they were to suffer would be the result of fifth column sabotage, perhaps the handiwork of hostile elements among their native labourers at their stores depots. To approach an enemy supply centre undetected, however, and plant time bombs would probably be impossible, so I decided to insert time bombs either into trucks on the move or when halted at staging areas.

We spent a week at Siwa practising various methods of planting bombs on vehicles on the move. It was found impossible to do so unless the vehicles were forced to slow down, in order to give the attacker sufficient time to emerge from a place of cover at the side of the road undetected and lob his bomb into the back of the truck. Some obstruction must therefore be placed in the road and for this purpose four large petrol drums and two long poles were taken with the Patrol for this operation, in addition to two red hurricane lamps and two large white notice boards. On each I wrote "ACHTUNG! STRASSENBAU". It seemed the right sort of "Road Under Repair" warning for drivers on the Via Balbia.

In the hope of deceiving any occupants who might be in the back of an enemy lorry, the bombs were wrapped in Italian haversacks, a consignment of which Bill Kennedy-Shaw, our Intelligence Officer, acquired for the purpose. A "time-pencil" (a form of delayed fuse) connected to the bomb protruded from a corner of the haversack. When the moment arrived the bomb-thrower would squueeze the end of the time-pencil to start the fusing process and then drop the haversack gently over the tail-board of the vehicle. The bombs themselves weighed two pounds, consisting of a mixture of high explosive and an incendiary substance, and were made fast to small tins of petrol. I thus visualized that the enemy lorry drivers and occupants would attach no significance either to the means by which they were forced to slow down or to the extra item of equipment bouncing in the back of the lorry. When the explosion came, half an hour or an hour to two hours later, depending on which type of time-pencil we employed, it would be a shattering surprise and an insoluble riddle for those who investigated the disaster. The scene of the explosion would be at a considerable and variable distance from the point on the road near Marble Arch where the traffic census was being conducted.

G.1 Patrol were to carry out this scheme between Marble Arch and Sirte, this is, west of the road-watch, while T.2 Patrol under Nick Wilder would do the same on the coastal road between Agedabia and Benghazi beyond the road-watch from me. In order that explosions would not occur as vehicles were passing the road-watch, G.1 would concentrate chiefly on west-bound vehicles and T.2 on east-bound. Nick Wilder did not want to see my bombs go off just where he was, nor did I want to see his.

After nearly a month's inactivity, therefore, G.1 Patrol set out on its long journey westward on 8 May heavily laden with jerricans of petrol, bombs, notice boards, hurricane lamps, poles and empty tar barrels. We refilled with petrol at Jarabub and again at the secret dump established north-east of Jalo on the edge of the sand sea. Shortly after leaving here our tyres gave us serious trouble. Goodyear and Dunlop tyres stood the strain fairly successfully of carrying 30-cwt trucks loaded to a capacity of three tons even on the hot sand, but a new type with which we had been issued cracked and burst at an anxious rate. It was difficult to keep the tyres at their proper pressure. The pressure would double in the course of two hours' running on the hot sand. In very soft going it was necessary to deflate the tyres. By the time we had passed north of Jalo we had very few to spare and the prospects of continuing the operation seemed hazardous. I decided therefore to retrieve some tyres from our old friend, the derelict Ford 30-cwt No.6, which I had abandoned for lack of oil four months previously among some dunes south of Ain Sidi Mohammed, eighty miles to the south of our route.

Leaving three trucks at the top of the escarpment, I went on with two trucks through the very difficult country of the depression. The latter part, across some small irregular dunes, was found impassable for our Chevrolets, although our Fords had earlier negotiated it when laden, though with difficulty, when finding a route south of Marada. We therefore dumped the loads of our trucks beneath a few lonely palm trees, leaving my soldier-servant Wann to guard our kit, manning a Vickers machine gun mounted on its tripod. With our trucks thus lightened, we eventually reached old No.6. It was still sitting in a hollow between some dunes which had considerably shifted in the lapse of a short time. Having secured five good tyres from it, we returned to Wann on his lonely vigil the next day, replaced the contents of our trucks and rejoined the rest of the Patrol of three trucks waiting for me to the north. It was fortunate that we had acquired these additional tyres for we had several more tyre bursts during the next three weeks. When we finally reached Siwa we had only one spare. Y.1 Patrol, with David Lloyd Owen, had had similar difficulties. They had left Siwa on the same day as ourselves for a trip even further west, but had had so many tyre bursts that they were obliged to turn back when about half way to their destination, abandoning their operation to form another secret dump fifty miles south of Marble Arch.

I planned to attack traffic at dusk in the early night in the area near Nofilia. The Marada-El Agheila road was crossed without incident and next day we met Gus Holliman and S.1 Patrol just returning from a spell of road-watch. Holliman gave us the latest news about the types and the density of enemy vehicles. Travelling in widely dispersed formation across very open rolling country of good hard going, we approached the main north road, the Via Balbia, where it crossed a wadi. We halted in the late afternoon sunshine on some high ground and could watch, as we sat in our trucks, heavy enemy traffic passing along an embankment and over a bridge. Tankers, staff cars, 5-ton lorries and trailers and occasionally guns were all roaring by and took no notice of the five trucks watching from the hillside a mile away. A few aircraft flew up and down the road.

In this region there is good cover in the small wadis close to the road, but the ground is open and featureless from four miles south of it. We moved off to hide up in one of these wadis, passing a few native encampments on the way. While the Patrol started to brew up and cook the evening meal, I went with the two navigators to watch the traffic until darkness came on. Then, returning to the Patrol myself, I sent Leach and Blaney, our navigators, to examine the road closely. They returned next morning having found a point where a large heap of small stones, deposited on the side for repair purposes, had spread across part of the surface. This should provide a suitable excuse for our "Strassenbau". On both sides was a bank and ditch and a few bushes. On the way home at night Leach and Blaney had come across a small camp of about twenty natives sitting round a fire quite close to our position. As far as they could see none of them wore the uniform of enemy native troops, although several of them had Italian greatcoats. During our first evening numerous natives took a lively interest in us. One guardsman said that he heard a native say, *"mush askeri Tedesci"*, ("not German troops"). As was to be expected, they were not friendly like the Senussi of Cyrenaica. No eggs were offered us. There were no dates for them.

We lay up all the next day until, in the later afternoon, a strong khamsin wind blowing from the south, we moved on in the evening a short distance into a wadi that descends directly to the road. We camped among some bushes in a deep water runnel and could see the traffic on the road from our position. That night we were to attack the road, synchronizing our attempt with that of T.2 Patrol, 160 miles further east.

At dusk we fitted the time-pencils to some bombs and placed them in the haversacks, and seven of us set off in one truck, my own. A fair quantity of vehicles was passing by. The truck was placed 150 yards from the road to give covering fire if required. Two men were stationed by the side of the road to give close support, while two more, one of them myself, would carry out the placing of the bombs at the road block. During a pause in the traffic we placed four barrels on the road around the pile of stones, which were shovelled further into the roadway, and placed the other paraphernalia in position. The first truck passed by very fast. We therefore moved the barrels and stones further across the road, but as the passing lorries still did not slow down we eventually pushed our road block so far across the surface that a large lorry would be almost obliged to pull off it.

I tried hiding behind one of the barrels. As a vehicle approached, its bright headlights lit up my shoulders on either side. The barrel was smaller than I had imagined. One lorry practically came to a standstill in the middle of the road block. The passenger inside peered down at me, but it went on without apparently taking any notice. Lorries frequently came along, one close behind the other, so that I would be lit up by the lights on the second lorry if I jumped up to put a bomb in the first. In dodging round the barrel, it was impossible to avoid being conspicuous either to the lorry that was passing or to its successor close behind. The only other alternative was for me to crouch behind the bank and then leap up as the vehicle passed, but this entailed crossing a small ditch and catching up with the truck. The enemy drivers, however, were very quick in getting under way each time they slowed down, and I failed to insert my bomb in this manner after several attempts, as did others of my Patrol who tried this method. It would have been fairly easy on occasions to have placed a bomb in a trailer, but I decided that this should not be done, since the drivers would be unaffected by the explosion, a highly desirable, if not essential, part of the ploy for mystifying the enemy. The height of the trucks presented an additional problem which meant *throwing* the bombs, rather clumsy missiles, whereas it had been intended to *drop* them in position.

By 2 a.m. we had had very little success. I had thrown only two bombs. The enemy were evidently very windy and not at all reassured by our excellent road block made in Siwa, but looking just like those made in their homelands. I decided now to try chasing enemy vehicles on the road in my truck, driving with no lights. The slight noise of our quiet Chevrolet engines would be drowned in the great volume of sound invariably made by the Diesel engines of our quarry. Lance-Sergeant Fraser sat on the bonnet with a bomb ready to throw into the back of a truck as I slowed down to close in on it.

We waited for the next lorry to come. Soon a lorry and trailer passed and I drove on to the road and started after it. Having gone a short way we came to our own road block which we had left in position, hoping to familiarize the enemy with this object like wild duck with a hide. We found a vehicle at the entrance to the road block. It was a lorry on tow to the previous lorry, which we had seen approaching. Two diminutive Italians came up to us shouting and gesticulating. Something, they said, was wrong with the engine. Their lorry had been on tow until the tow rope had broken when the towing lorry, travelling at great speed, had swerved to pass through the obstruction. It was difficult to know what to do with our victims and their transport. The Italians obviously took us for Germans for they tried to speak to me in broken German, explaining that they wished us to tow them to Sirte. While I made a hasty and fruitless attempt to make their vehicle work, thinking it would be useful to us as a stalking horse, to be used at this game in daylight, some of our men treated our two momentary allies somewhat brusquely. I went back to my truck and ordered them to be released and the contents of their pockets restored. Wann was their temporary jailer and he handed them back to me. Such treatment was apparently to be expected at the hands of their Teuton allies and their continued affable manner did not betray any suspicion that we were anything else than prototypes of their more arrogant partner.

I pointed out to them in my almost negligible Italian that there

94

was an Italian lorry coming on behind us which would help them, and indeed the lights on an oncoming lorry were approaching. We regretted that our business was too urgent to warrant further delay. By this means I hoped that the lorry behind us would tow them and their truck away from a neighbourhood embarrassing to us and at the same time the enemy would be none the wiser. To take them prisoner and tow their truck off the road would undoubtedly draw suspicion the next day when the derelict lorry would be seen or the men found missing and a search made. We parted therefore with loud expressions of *"Grazie Kamarade"* on their part. Squeezing past their truck and our road block, we continued along the road westward.

We were looking about, as we went along, for a more suitable site for a road block the next night not too near where we were now. A lorry and trailer drawn up on the side of the road was passed after three miles and then one of our tyres burst. I told the driver to turn off the road in order to change the wheel, only to find that he had neglected to mend the spare tyre which had been punctured on the previous day. We were now about eight miles from the remainder of the Patrol and dawn would be on us soon. There was no sign of the vehicle which we had seen travelling behind us so we presumed it had stopped to help the two Italians. We drove with the flat tyre for about three miles away from the road making a lot of noise as I dodged between the hillocks in first gear. Here we camouflaged the truck and three of us set off on foot for the Patrol to obtain help, leaving four with the truck. As dawn broke I could see that the traffic on the road was starting to increase and the inopportune Italian truck was still stuck in the same place where the road crossed the bottom of our wadi. Enemy traffic was somewhat congested, having difficulty in passing it. Still, all seemed quiet at the top of our little valley. I sent Corporal Findlay off with one truck to rescue No.1 (my truck), then had some breakfast and an hour's sleep. Findlay returned with my truck and four men at about 11 a.m. They could have been seen from the main road, but one could not help that.

Two hours later we were having our lunch; in fact, I was just adding the luxury of some Cairo cream to a tinned peach when Sutton, who was on sentry, came dashing up. Enemy with transport, it appeared, had come over the side of the wadi towards us. They were apparently following the tracks of No.1 and Findlay's truck. In spite of our good camouflage they spotted us, probably remarking our wireless aerial rigged up for the midday call to Siwa. I ordered the gunners to stand to just as the enemy started to open fire. Matthews was killed as he jumped on top of his truck to man his gun, a bullet striking his forehead. It was some time before our own gunners could open fire on account of the camouflage which impeded them from getting at their guns, and in reaching them one was bound to expose oneself to the enemy fire, which was fairly brisk. At first I could not see exactly where this was coming from, but I soon caught sight of several enemy crawling about 150 yards away. They were attacking us from the top of the wadi and closing in on the hill-sides round us. I felled one with a rifle as he approached with a bunch of others on the hillside. They were Italians and we blazed away at any we saw and at the sound of their machine guns. The two water-cooled Vickers guns manned by Duncalfe and Wann kept up a good steady patter and the fast-firing Vickers "K" and the double Browning poured out streams of lead. I and some others, armed with grenades, moved over to our left waiting for the enemy near the topmost truck, expecting them to assault from the close cover down the water runnel. Gradually their fire became less intense.

After the engagement had lasted twenty minutes I ordered the three lower trucks, which could get out of the wadi fairly easily and were furthest from the enemy, to leave by our only remaining line of retreat, up a small subsidiary river bed. The remaining two trucks, which were deep in the water runnel, kept up their heavy fire and the three trucks made off one by one, still firing as they went. The enemy fire slackened. Before they reorganized for a new attack I must get all the Patrol away. The sides of the runnel were five foot high where the last two trucks were stranded. My own, No.1, was backed along the narrow river bed and was driven away. Truck No. 5, driven by Corporal Inwood, the last to leave, had a good deal of trouble. Every time it tried to climb the banks of the runnel heavy bursts of machine-gun fire sprayed it. Two of us continued firing from the ground and jumped on to it as Inwood drove away. Guardsman Findlay's truck, which had led the way out, had come upon about twenty Italian soldiers. The crew had fired on them and they had gone to ground without returning our fire;

probably a fair number of them had been hit. Two of our trucks, including mine, were found waiting for us a few hundred yards up the small wadi and two more a mile further on.

All this had taken place within view of the main road with its stream of traffic and one felt that at any moment considerable enemy reinforcements could be brought up. It was early afternoon, with seven hours of daylight ahead. We must therefore make off to the south hoping to elude pursuit. Aircraft would probably be after us soon. They would expect us to make off in a south-easterly direction, that is more or less towards our home, though several hundred miles away. We therefore set off towards the south-west, changing our course frequently in an attempt to lose our tracks, in very open formation and going as fast as we could.

No enemy aircraft, however, were seen and, after travelling sixty-five miles, we camped among some small dunes and scrub in the middle of a large open plain. Each truck was responsible for guarding a section of our perimeter. Guardsman Matthews was buried on the southern side of a conspicuous hill. A message was sent to Headquarters reporting the incident and permission was granted, now that our presence was discovered, to raid the road further west. Nick Wilder had had no better results than I had. Wireless communication was difficult as the Wyndham aerial had been broken by the enemy's fire during our recent engagement. Stewart, our signaller for this trip, showed great skill in carrying on with the short rod aerial. I was not listening in when he said, "I think I have Siwa now, Sir". So I took the second pair of phones: "Oh! You mean that little piping under the noisy one?" "No, Sir I mean the one weaker than that. I think it is Barbour at the other end."

I decided to wait for five days before our proposed raid as there was almost no moon at present. By 21 May the moon would not set until 1 a.m. The enemy never showed signs of following us during our stay. Only one reconnaissance aircraft flew over. We spent some time looking for the petrol dumped by David Lloyd Owen, but it was so skilfully hidden that we could not find it in spite of passing within a few yards of it, as I learned later. After three days we moved off to a new camp site fifty miles further west, which was to be a base for our attack. One truck, the brakes of which did not function well, was left here with Guardsman Waiting and Private Astle, the medical orderly. I gave them instructions that, if I could not find the rendezvous on returning from the raid in the dark, I would fire white and green Very lights when in the neighbourhood, and they would fire green ones to guide me to the position.

We left about midday on 21 May, crossing the open ground towards the north so as to arrive near the road by sunset. A "Casa Cantieri" or roadhouse was selected as the main target for our attack, since enemy vehicles were in the habit of halting at such places during the hours of darkness. On approaching the main road we met with difficult going: small barriers of sand dunes and hummocks, such as are often found near the sea shore. The steering of No.2, the wireless truck, broke when close to the road. To repair this would take considerable time and we therefore towed the truck back and camped about ten miles south of the road, putting off the raid until the following night. That day we repaired the steering, a few aircraft were seen and in the evening we set off for the road again, about six miles away. As we reached it two vehicles passed. While Sergeant Fraser supervised a party which laid mines in the surface and verges of the road, using pick axes, I swarmed up a telegraph pole and cut the wires. The lights of some oncoming traffic could be seen in the distance. All six wires were eventually cut, each falling with a twang on to the road below. We then mounted our trucks and drove onto the road, heading eastwards with headlights full on.

The white buildings of the roadhouse were soon lit up by our headlamps and numbers of lorries stood parked on both sides of the road outside. According to plan we drove slowly on. As we came among the lorries and opposite the buildings we let fly with all our machine guns. The two rear trucks also threw time bombs and grenades into them and into the midst of a number of enemy soldiers standing about. The blaze of our fire was tremendous, our different calibre guns firing tracer, incendiary, armour-piercing and high explosive. As we left, one truck was burning and the others considerably damaged. The last of our trucks, which went round the back of the roadhouse, was unfortunately temporarily lost and we waited for it for some time a mile further down the road. Here we laid more mines and Guardsman Campbell swarmed up a pole and cut all the telephone wires again. We could hear our missing truck moving about among the sand dunes south of the road so we chased after it. For an hour we searched for it but could not find it. When on the move, you could not hear its engine.

By this time the moon was nearly setting. We heard and saw the glow of two heavy explosions as some enemy vehicles must have detonated our mines on the road and several lesser explosions denoted time bombs going off in the lorries. I made off southward with the three trucks, sticking in the soft sand dunes several times. As the moon had now set we used our headlights again. We were much delayed in negotiating a deep wadi with high scrub and did not reach the good hard going further south until an hour before dawn. Here we made rapid progress. We picked up our outward tracks by first light and followed them back to our rendezvous, forty miles inland.

There was no sign here of the truck lost at the Casa Cantieri, and, worse still, Waiting and Astle had disappeared, though their truck and kit were still there. Eventually they were seen in the distance walking rapidly away. We again expected to see enemy aircraft soon after dawn, so we camouflaged the trucks carefully. The missing truck arrived as we were having breakfast, but there was no further sign of Waiting and Astle, who, we thought, would soon return after their apparent uneasiness at our approach. We searched for them that morning with one truck but could not find them, and in the afternoon the whole Patrol, moving in extended line, scoured the country around. I left two trucks at a point in the direction of which they were last seen walking and returned to the rendezvous. Here I could see the foot-prints of the missing men, who had apparently returned in our absence in search of food and water. It was now too dark to search for them and we spent all night lighting huge bonfires and letting off Very lights at the two different points where our Patrol was camped. The next day with two trucks we visited a second emergency rendezvous further south, leaving some water there and at several other points, though we were very short of it ourselves.

Eventually their tracks were picked up heading north. We could slowly follow these wherever they led over soft going, but we continually lost them on hard ground. All day we continued to track them slowly until it grew dark. We drove on in the darkness and set up a cairn with a can of water and a note telling them for heavens sake to keep still and not to go on walking. On our way back to camp we saw a small light in the darkness. We drove up to it. It was them. They thought they were giving themselves up to an enemy force. The two men had walked forty-five miles in two days with a quarter of a water bottle between them; the sandals they were wearing, as we knew from their tracks, had broken and they had been walking with torn up clothing wound round their feet.

The next day, 25 May, we started home. It had been very hot during the last week and our water tanks had leaked considerably. The water we had left was somewhat in the nature of soup in colour, temperature and consistency. Small dead butterflies gave it a special flavour. We had been on half-rations for a week, and now we had only 1½ gallons per man to see us and our vehicles home, six hundred odd miles away. We crossed the Marada road without incident, passed north of Jalo, now enemy-held, at good speed and eventually reached Jarabub. Even the bad water there was welcome. The following day we reached Siwa, two days after the return of G.2 Patrol from Benghazi.

Chapter 6

ROMMEL TRIUMPHANT

8th Army's Gazala Line position consisted of strongly fortified "boxes" fronted by minefields. Rommel attacked with a right hook round the desert flank. Heavy tank battles followed with fluctuating fortunes. Eventually 8th Army was forced to retire. Nothing came of a plan to hold a line incorporating Tobruk, and the town was once more left isolated. Rommel promptly attacked and captured it – a disaster for British arms. Now 8th Army streamed back to the Alamein position well inside Egypt and prepared to conquer or die.

The LRDG, while maintaining their basic road-watch on the Via Balbia, were also heavily involved in SAS operations designed to harass the advancing German-Italian army. They lost their base at Siwa and Alastair Timpson lost his close friend and second-in-command, Robin Gurdon.

The news of the battle being fought on the Gazala line was favourable at first. With optimistic expectations that the scene of the fighting would soon move westward into our own operation area, both "G" Patrols left for Cyrenaica. My G.1, after a week's interlude at base, took to the road again on 6 June and our activities will be described shortly.

G.2, under Robin Gurdon, set off on 8 June to take David Stirling and three of his parties to destroy aircraft at Benina and the two Berka aerodromes, all near Benghazi. Again Stirling had his "Blitzwagon". Near Trigh el Abd the "Blitzwagon" and one of G.2's trucks hit thermos bombs. Two trucks under Corporal Wilson were sent back to Siwa to bring up a party to repair them while the remainder continued north.

Three nights after leaving Siwa the SAS parties were duly dropped near their targets and the Patrol lay up all day without incident. That night, the night for the concerted SAS attack, an unpleasant surprise was sprung by the RAF who bombed Benghazi, dropping their bright flares and arousing the entire ground defence.

Stirling returned with his party next morning having been successful at Benina aerodrome, but there was no sign yet of Mayne's party and the Free French party, both of which attacked Berka. The following morning, however, these parties reached the rendezvous, though they had casualties, one wounded and one missing. They had had much difficulty in carrying out their tasks on account of the activities of the RAF. Stirling was much annoyed as the RAF were supposed to have given Benghazi a miss on that particular night. A Junkers 87 circled round the area that day, but did not discover the Patrol.

After hiding up for another day in the hope that the missing man would return, the Patrol moved off a short distance north-ward. Stirling and some of his party drove on to the main road toward Benghazi in the hope of renewing his attempt of the previous month to destroy shipping in the main harbour. On this occasion, however, the enemy took careful precautions. The party was lucky to escape from a highly suspicious traffic control post at Benina, and then proceeded to destroy any vehicles they could find on the road between there and Benghazi. They were chased by some enemy forces, but escaped in the dark. However, they lost their truck and nearly their lives by an accident. This occurred through somebody stepping on a time-pencil without having realized it. Some time later, when the safety fuse started to burn, the occupants fortunately realized their predicament from the smell of a burning fuse. Everyone hastily abandoned the truck before it disintegrated with the explosion of all the bombs it contained. The truck was one borrowed from my Patrol.

Meanwhile Robin Gurdon and a party of the Patrol had mined the El Abiar railway again and returned to camp. Here the Patrol lay up all day. Next morning a ME 110 caused some anxiety by systematically quartering the country around. Senussi natives also reported that the Italians had established a post close by. As Stirling had not turned up, and as he had lost his truck, Robin Gurdon went on with a small party on foot to a place indicated by a Senussi, where he found David and his men resting in a cave. Everyone walked back to the trucks which Robin had left. They moved off at dusk to the south.

The broken-down staff car and the truck damaged near the Trigh el Abd on the outward journey had meanwhile been repaired by a party from Siwa. They were now picked up and the Patrol continued its journey homeward. Travelling fast they reached Siwa on 21 June.

G.1 Patrol with myself had meanwhile set off on 6 June to take over from David Lloyd Owen a road-watch covering the inland tracks west of Mekili, where there was supposed to be some enemy traffic. The camp site for this road-watch was set in a shallow basin, and so well was it concealed that we had much difficulty in finding it. Two men of Y.1 Patrol in fact saw us first from their look-out and led us to the camp site. From a hundred yards away the trucks were indistinguishable from large thorn bushes.

David Lloyd Owen had seen no enemy traffic during the week he spent there. No enemy traffic moved in our vicinity when I was there either and this job was worse than dull as the physical discomforts were most unpleasant. Not a breath of air stirred this scorching part of the desert all morning and noon, and in the late afternoon a hot breeze would blow the soft sand from off the old tracks. Camels had at some time previously used this area, and former advances and retreats had passed by, leaving in their wake old slit trenches and the refuse of leaguer sites. It was hell to us but a paradise for flies.

If we had had to stay in this area several weeks I think we would have all gone insane. Even individually the fly of the Middle East is a much more offensive creature than the house fly of England. Instead of buzzing around by the window or beneath the central light as the innocuous house flies do at home, the fly of Africa is intent on nosing its way into the eyes, ears and nose. In swarms, as they were here, the flies were as powerfully obnoxious as Gulliver's multitudes of Lilliputians, but far more evil. It was impossible for any man to be on sentry for more than half an hour without risk of his becoming unreliable, if not mad. It was too hot to eat more than a little tinned fruit during the day, and then it was a question of swallowing flies along with the food. All this might seem unimportant, but it was very real at the time, and equalled any morbid theme of Conan Doyle or Edgar Allan Poe.

The monotony and the nightmare were broken at times by the activities of "A" Squadron, Middle East Commandos, under Major Knowles. They had established a forward base near our area and we held a supply of reserve petrol for them. They set forth with eighteen trucks in an attempt to raid the main roads in the Jebel to the north. In the first attempt they lost six trucks by the action of enemy aircraft, and in the second, a few days later, nearly all the rest the same way. We contacted them on two occasions and brought back some of their survivors whom we had seen being strafed not far from us. Enemy aircraft were plentiful and the only asset of the flies was they they made it difficult for us to hear them.

We received orders to investigate the Cheruba track and also another track to the south, which provided a welcome respite. Another duty to be discharged was to deliver half a million lire to another patrol, which in turn passed it on to Major Peniakoff, who was still engaged in bribing his way around the hill country near Martuba in the Jebel. All the while, too, the booming of the guns was heard to the east. Sometimes it seemed to be coming closer and we hoped to see signs of Rommel's army in retreat as it had been six months earlier. And then later the noise grew more indistinct and messages from Siwa confirmed that the battle of the Cauldron and Knightsbridge was going badly. Scores of dive-bombers would pass over on their way to Bir Hakeim and Tobruk and one wished one could do something to stop them. At last we were given welcome orders suspending the road-watch and instructing us to interfere more actively in the battle to the east.

R.2 Patrol under Croucher was sent to join me for this purpose. It was thought that the main enemy supply route was along the Afraq track, near Tmimi. We were to destroy their traffic here. We set off therefore first south and then east and finally north to circumvent Mekili. Both patrols were under my command and we travelled with G.1 Patrol in front and R.2 about twelve miles behind, for the sake of dispersal.

We lay up for one night south-east of Mekili and continued next day northward towards Afraq, situated on the edge of the hills. We had to pass close to Mekili, two hundred feet high, which stands on a hill rising solitary from the plain. Minefields

14. The Old Fort at Siwa. In the foreground are a Chevrolet and a Ford truck.

15. Siwa (see pp. 43-44)

16. The LRDG Heavy Section at Siwa, March 1942 (*IWM HU16585*).

17. Kufra: " The oasis was a stronghold of the Sudan Defence Force" (*p.28*).

18. Chevrolet in eroded landscape.

19. Somewhere north of Kufra.

20. On road watch (*IWM E12434*).

21. Chevrolet 30-cwt truck in a sand sea (*IWM HU16487*).

22. Chevrolets in a wadi (*IWM E12384*).

23. Truck bogged in sand (*IWM E12393*).

24. Camouflaged truck (*IWM E12403*).

25. Ford truck stuck in the sand (*IWM HU16489*).

26. Dunes, one to two hundred feet high, in a sand sea (*IWM HU16566*).

27. On the move on good going (*IWM HU16488*).

28. Patrol on good going (*IWM HU16490*).

29. Enemy vehicles on the Via Balbia (*IWM E12435*).

prevented us from giving it a wide berth. Large native encampments were passed near here. Occasionally the dust of distant enemy trucks could be seen to the north and aircraft flew by now and then. A ME 109 turned towards us and circled round us several times. We carried out all the tricks of pretending we were good friends, changing our direction to the less suspicious one of due east, as if we were heading towards El Adem near Tobruk. He left us after a while and luckily did not spot the other Patrol travelling behind us. Just as we were tucking into the bottom of a wadi in the foothills he flew over us again, making for Martuba, their main fighter aerodrome seven miles away. During the two hours before dark we fully expected a pack of them to come back after us, but night came at last and nothing happened. R.2 Patrol arrived after half an hour.

After negotiating some difficult country we investigated the Afraq track and waited on it for some time, but no enemy transport came by. As we learnt later, the enemy had now shifted his communications to the main north road only. The battle of the Cauldron was now over and he was closing in on Tobruk. I found Martuba airfield had been evacuated. We decided to attack the main road west of Martuba and moved off in the dark to a point a few miles from it which we reached at dawn, and camped there for the day. This was a comparatively thickly populated area and many natives came to us to discuss the military situation. Several of them knew Major Peniakoff, who was operating nearby. They reported also the presence of various enemy camps in the area. We could hear meanwhile some traffic passing along the main road. Aircraft as usual were plentiful and forbade movement during the day.

Towards dusk we turned on to a subsidiary road which took us down to the main road. As we approached an occasional vehicle passed, but soon none came by at all. Both Patrols ranged their trucks along one side of the road and waited for the first victim to pass. After about an hour two Italian lorries, tank transporters, came by with M13 tanks. The firing of my gun was the signal for all the others to let fly. For the space of a minute the air was full of the roar and flash of machine guns. R.2 Patrol stopped the leading transporter with their fire and my Patrol dealt with the second, two men in the front being killed and two, who were inside the tank, were taken prisoner. Various other occupants escaped in the dark and we could hear them shouting on the far side of the road. I inspected the first transporter and tank and found one dead man in the front and one wounded in the back.

Meanwhile a truck approaching us from the east had stopped two miles down the road and no more traffic was coming from the west. I made an abortive search for the escaped enemy across the road, but shortly afterwards a civil war between the two Patrols developed when they became split up in the darkness. For a while both Patrols shot at one another, without casualties, yet badly spoiling the party. Mistaking each other for the enemy, we eventually drew off in different directions. As only too many soldiers have found to their cost, when comparatively large numbers of men are employed in the dark without careful rehearsal, the fighting is apt to become confused.

Expecting to be followed, next day we took careful precautions in retracing and losing our tracks during the night, hiding up in a small wadi beneath some olive trees. Here we received orders to return home since conditions at Siwa were now becoming precarious. There was much aircraft activity. We had to negotiate some difficult country among the foothills north of Mekili. Eventually, heading southward, we passed Mekili on the west side and so home to Siwa, arriving there on 22 June.

At Siwa it was difficult to keep up to date with the fast-moving events in the north. 8th Army was naturally busy with matters of greater importance than the activities of our small unit. By the time I reached Siwa we knew that 8th Army was withdrawing on Matruh and might have to retire even further. This would leave Siwa well west of our main forces. We never had been prepared to defend the oasis ourselves, for our Patrols were used entirely for long distance work and never for our own self-protection. Hurried plans now had to be made to provide what defence we could against rapid enemy action before we could evacuate our stores and the whole paraphernalia of Group Headquarters. A Patrol guarded the main approach to the oasis and the rest were disposed as a mobile reserve ready for action within fifteen minutes.

Yet we still had certain commitments. The road-watch near El Agheila must be maintained, so certain patrols were detailed to go west in succession to complete their allotted spell on road-watch and then return, not to Siwa, but to Kufra, as base for their future activities.

Colonel Guy Prendergast called a conference. A large map of the Middle East was spread out and the various possibilities were discussed as to where the LRDG would set up its headquarters. To go east of the Nile was one suggestion; the humorist or pessimist who made it, however, was rebuked. Robin Gurdon, in Coldstream fashion, suggested Mustafa Barracks, Alexandria, and I represented the Scots Guards' interest by proposing the Citadel at Cairo. But Colonel Guy decided that we would make a temporary headquarters somewhere just west of Alexandria near the sea where he found a place marked on the map which no one had ever heard of: El Alamein. Next day the various elements of Headquarters started to evacuate Siwa, followed later by some of the patrols, including G.2 with Robin Gurdon on 25th June, and finally G.1 and I on 28th June.

We travelled northwards, not to Matruh for this was considered unsafe, but by a more easterly route through Qara, at the western end of the Qattara Depression, and thence northward through Baggush on the coast. Thirty miles south of the latter we ran into a part of the German Army. Some armoured cars followed us for a while, but it was not difficult to escape in the heat-haze of midday. We travelled thirty miles eastward parallel with the coast and then turned north. This time we met the British Army. The first part of it that we contacted was much troubled by our appearance. A long column of lorries was jogging eastwards across the horizon. They halted when we drew near. Leaving my Patrol, I drove along up to the nearest P/U to find the commander of this supply column pointing his revolver and ready to sell his life dearly. Civil war was, however, averted and the Patrol drove northward making for the main road.

All that afternoon, from twenty-five miles inland up to the coast, we passed through hundreds of straggling lines of our yellow 8th Army vehicles, each heading eastward on its allotted course. In the heat-haze they resembled yellow houses spread across the horizon. A few ME 109s were diving from the skies like birds of prey. But our own fighters were there too and we felt very safe as we enjoyed the novel experience of having our own fighter cover.

The main North Road was thick with traffic, but, travelling at speed and overtaking trucks the whole time, we reached the familiar region of Daba in the later afternoon, hoping to have news of the 201st Guards Motor Brigade (as it was now styled). 8th Army Headquarters was temporarily established here and we learnt the brief details of recent events. We heard about Rigel Ridge where my own Battalion had lost heavily. Nothing was yet known of the Coldstream's escape from Tobruk. We only knew that Tobruk had fallen, that Matruh was surrounded and being evacuated, and that we were withdrawing to Alamein. One desperate staff officer asked if we had seen a train he had sent off that morning to Matruh and which he now could not stop. John Haselden, as G(1) Intelligence, was there too, cheerful and confident as ever. General Auchinleck was also there, having personally taken over the Army's command. In spite of the huge evacuation eastward back to a point so near to the last ditch that it must have appeared a rout to the outside world, there was in fact no chaos and no pessimism.

After I had been introduced to him by John Haselden, General Auchinleck explained, in confident manner, how he was withdrawing to the narrow area between the Qattara Depression and Alamein on the coast. He in turn introduced me to Brigadier Hugh Mainwaring, his acting Chief of Staff at Advance Headquarters, as they were worried about the garrison of Australian troops and two hundred and fifty vehicles still at Jarabub. Mainwaring wanted me to go back to Siwa and then the ninety miles further west to Jarabub and lead the Australians safely back through the Qattara Depression via the precarious Kunaitra Crossing near Qara. When I replied that I must obtain my orders from my own commanding officer, he readily agreed. He would speak to Guy Prendergast, who I said should be somewhere near the railway station at Alamein by now. I would be there early next day and would explain the problem.

We continued along the road at dusk and through the night by the light of the moon. Enemy aircraft were fairly active bombing and strafing the road all night. We did not attempt to keep the Patrol together, except that the trucks must travel by pairs and meet at a certain rendezvous. Our medical orderly was called upon to make good use of his knowledge on one occasion when his truck came upon a number of casualties caused by one of these enemy raids. At about two in the morning we eventually reached the new camp site of our Headquarters, and after a short sleep we breakfasted there with G.2 Patrol next morning.

I had brought the instructions from Army Headquarters for a

Patrol to be sent to extricate the garrison at Jarabub by way of the Qattara Depression. Colonel Guy ordered Gus Holliman with Rhodesian S.1 Patrol to do the job (he did this with the loss of only three vehicles in the swampy ground of Kunaitra, keeping south of the Depression to Farafra Oasis and Fayoum). I then paid a short visit to my Battalion, or rather the remnants of it, camped near Amariya, but was recalled, after spending an hour there, to receive orders for a new operation. John Haselden had come with instructions from the Army Commander. It was essential to destroy vital enemy supplies on their lines of communication at this critical stage in the 8th Army's existence. David Stirling arrived in the evening with new plans for destroying enemy aircraft which would involve both SAS and LRDG patrols. The two next operations of both "G" Patrols were to entail operating under David's command.

On 1 July, the day after we had reached our temporary headquarters near Alamein, G.1 Patrol and I left to operate against enemy communications near the battle front under LRDG command, since Stirling's plan had not yet matured. We had not had much rest ever since our month's inactivity in April. This summer had not been so hot as that of the previous year; nevertheless, lack of sleep at night which we spent on the move, and the heat during the day while we lay under our camouflaged trucks in the company of lizards and scorpions seeking shade, and the insistent swarm of flies, had had their effect. Sometimes scorpions sought warmth. I was getting out of my sleeping bag one morning when one of the black variety popped out from under my chin and scuttled away, obviously grateful for a warm night tucked up next to me. I was never bitten by a scorpion, but some of us were. Guardsman "Pongo" Reid was obviously an attraction for them. He was bitten six times when with me, but he had practically no reaction from his bites. Several cases of dysentery developed during the next operation, Corporal Leach being particularly bad. Sergeant Fraser developed jaundice and could be given no treatment. I myself had impetigo, with bandages round my face, when we started. Nearly everyone had bad desert sores. The business in hand, however, was urgent. Even if a rest had been possible, no one would have liked to remain inactive at this critical phase.

John Haselden visited us from Army Headquarters, and explained in more detail the nature of our mission. By withdrawing right back to Alamein we were forcing the enemy to over-reach himself, to outrun his supplies. His forward elements were particularly short of water and petrol, or rather the means of bringing these forward. It was our object therefore to make water-trucks and water-points, tankers and petrol-points our targets. We in G.1 Patrol would leave with Y.2 Patrol, under Anthony Hunter, call at Army Headquarters for latest information, and then go through the semi-stabilized Alamein Line. After this, G.1 would attack targets between the Alamein Line and Matruh, while Y.2 would do the same further west.

We set off in the early morning of 1 July. We had five 30-cwt trucks, Y.2 had four. We learnt at Army headquarters and then at 13th Corps headquarters, where we met Bernard Bruce on the staff of General John Harding, that some forward elements of the enemy had bumped our line for the first time. That morning twenty tanks had been repulsed in the north. Our reconnaissance aircraft reported a large number of armoured fighting vehicles in the extreme south, but the enemy was not yet prepared to launch any determined attack. This gave us time to stabilize the fluid state in which we had been ever since the retreat from Gazala, and consolidate our defence on ground of our own choosing. The enemy was not slow in contesting this choice.

In spite of the large tank force reported to be in that area, I considered that the southern end of the line immediately north of the Qattara Depression offered the best chance of passing through to the west undetected. We drove past various units on the way southward. We saw the New Zealand Division digging in; we could not find 1st Armoured Divisional Head-quarters, but met a South African armoured car squadron and the remnants of a supply column of 4th Indian Division which had escaped from Matruh. To the west of us now, overlooking the Qattara Depression, was a high feature, Naqb Abu Dweis, on which could be seen, in the light of dawn, some troops and transport. We were told they were part of the 9th Indian Brigade.

That day I did not take the steering wheel, but let Guardsman Campbell drive. We drove down a track towards the feature, coming from the north-east, but found the way mined and wired. Two shells landed close, but these, I thought, were stray shots from a battle going on in the north. I drew back, had breakfast and observed that the hill was still occupied. I then drove on, nine vehicles in line ahead, toward Abu Dweis again, approaching it from a new angle. As we came closer, men on top of the hill started to run about and drive vehicles off it; then we came into dead ground. We rounded a corner on the track 300 yards from the base of the feature. Numerous vehicles stood about, chiefly yellow 8th Army colour. An armoured car of German appearance faced us on the track 100 yards away. As I halted to look through my field glasses Campbell spotted a full kitbag, a rifle and other forms of loot, and promptly descended from the truck to claim the reward of the opportunist. The moment, however, was not well chosen. Small arms fire opened up on us from all over the place. Two men jumped out of the armoured car and started to fire at us from the ground beside it. Not expecting trouble, my own gunners were not prepared, and in any case we had no intention of firing on our presumed friends, the Indian Brigade, even if the latter were mistakenly showing their independence in no uncertain manner. Campbell finally got back into his seat and from a sitting target we soon became a moving one. I signalled to the rest of the Patrol to turn about and Y.2 Patrol in the rear did the same. Artillery soon joined in the one-sided shooting match, their shells landing among us and whistling by in profusion. I paused briefly behind a small ridge after nearly a mile, but the shelling did not in the least abate and continued to follow us as we rushed back across the open plain. We paused at last when out of range. Only one truck had been slightly damaged. Anthony's Patrol had taken a different line of retreat and we did not see them until we met at our rendezvous at Ain Tartura, a hundred miles south of Matruh, a few days later. He got through the line further north the night of the following day. At the time I still thought we had possibly been fired on by our own forces, but later we learnt they were, in fact, Germans with a considerable quantity of captured British transport.

I now decided to make a long detour by way of the Qattara Depression. This area was very little known at the time. It had previously been considered impassable, and no doubt it is in winter; yet it was to provide, for the next three months, the high road for incursions by LRDG and SAS behind the Alamein Line. On this particular trip we made many mistakes through lack of geographical information. We sought to find a way up the huge escarpment that bounds the depression to the north and became very badly bogged in doing so. The large slabs of cracked mud are very treacherous. At times one can bump slowly along over them with impunity, and then one suddenly subsides, the truck resting on its chassis while the wheels grind in the water below.

After three days we eventually reached the small oasis of Qara at the western end where the water is bad but a fair number of natives live in white-painted mud houses perched high on a precipitous hill. The telephone line to Siwa, only fifty miles away, still worked, and we discovered that the enemy had not occupied it yet. At Qara the mighty escarpment descends, for a while, to the plain. Here we could therefore go north at last, and then north-east to the rendezvous at Tartura above Qattara Spring, where we met Anthony Hunter and Y.2. He had been there nearly two days.

We now both had to wait, for our orders had been changed. David Stirling, with a large force of SAS piloted by G.2 Patrol and Gurdon, was on his way to meet with us here. All three LRDG Patrols would come under his command, both "G" Patrols and Y.2 under Anthony Hunter. Our role would be to pilot and help to transport his various parties in their raids on aeorodromes and communications, and do some additional raiding ourselves.

The next day, in the afternoon, a great cloud of dust could be seen approaching from the east. The country here is full of escarpments and clefts, and one could see the dust and hear the sound of vehicles long before they hove into view. Robin was in the lead with G.2 Patrol. We directed them to a hide-out next to our own. Then came truck after truck of SAS, first swarms of jeeps, then 3-tonners, and David in his famous staff car "Blitzwagon", Corporal Cooper, his inseparable gunner, beside him. Mayne, Fraser, Jellicoe, Mather and Scratchley were all there. Rawnsley was wearing a virgin-blue veil and azure pyjamas; here was the counterpart to Glubb's Arab Legion ("Glubb's Girls") in the west. Trucks raced to and fro churning up the powdery ground, until most of them came to rest after a while in a hollow half a mile away which I had recommended to them. As aircraft had been flying about we did not quite approve of all this crowded activity. Yet they had gone through the Alamein Line undetected; a ME 110 which now flew over took no notice and the reckless cheerfulness of our companions was stimulating.

Having to rely chiefly on LRDG wireless communications, and on our navigators, David kept our operators busy sending and receiving messages for the whole party. We had a conference that evening and again the next morning, in which he revealed his plans and gave his orders.

8th Army was about to begin a counter-offensive – completely abortive, as it turned out – and I doubt if most of those with the main forces were so much as aware of it. But we, at any rate, took it seriously, and with the optimism which fresh hopes for a renewed offensive so easily revived. It was hoped to drive the enemy beyond Daba, Fuka, Baggush, Matruh and even beyond Sollum, the frontier. Enemy fighters on landing grounds were our first priority target. At the initial stages of the offensive they would be chiefly at Daba and Fuka, well forward, but gradually they would be forced back. Parties of SAS would attack them in the area where they now were and would be ready to pounce on them, or as many as survived the first attacks, as they withdrew westwards. By the time they were driven back to the frontier there should be very few left. Naturally, reserves being brought up would be pounced on too. David's plans were nothing if not comprehensive. Traffic provided a subsidiary target. Even though such plans were never fully realized, amazing results were obtained. By aiming, with full energy of purpose, at 400 per cent success, David would obtain 100% results judged by normal estimates. In the course of the operations covering this period, eighty-five enemy aircraft, besides other targets, were destroyed. David, at the end of it, was furious that it was not more.

Anyone who wants to know the full story of David Stirling should read Virginia Cowles' book *The Phantom Major*. I found him a truly remarkable leader of men. Montgomery initially distrusted him, saying, "The boy Stirling is mad", but he soon changed his attitude.

David Stirling was not a snob, although he was apt to "go straight to the top" in order to get important things accomplished. He liked to deal with people who said "Yes" or "No", preferably not "No". Those who wanted to take a lot of time in coming to a decision angered him. And there nearly always was something he wanted done – and in a hurry. In the war it was a question of speedy destruction of the enemy – mainly the Germans. He had extraordinarily little fear, largely because he was so pre-occupied with how to execute an operation he was engaged in or because he was planning a new one. He also had enormous self-confidence. He was very lucky, not only in not getting bullets in him when engaged in a fight or on one of his many attempts at escape as a prisoner of war, but he was also lucky with many motor-car accidents and having luck in meeting rescuers. When he was finally captured for the second time in southern Tunisia, it was entirely through lack of fear and an obsession with destroying enemy aircraft. He had been at large for a day or two when he came upon a big aerodrome. He could not resist the temptation to reconnoitre it with a view to attacking it once he had got back to his main forces, which he had ample scope for doing. He had chanced his luck a bit too far. Later, when he had two Italian soldiers guarding him at a railway station, he knocked their heads together so hard that they lost him, but he was very lucky not to be brought down by all the subsequent firing from other troops. His luck ran out when he was at large in Austria being hidden by villagers at the top of a lonely valley. The Germans made an unexpected visit and he had to give himself up to save the villagers.

I and others will continue to admire and to wonder at David, and will relish his effrontery with the game of life, its hazards and its opportunities.

About midday Y.2 under Tony Hunter set off with three SAS parties for west of Fuka, G.1 and I with two SAS parties for Sidi Barrani, a long way west, and G.2 with Stirling and some of his men for the Fuka area. That was the last time I saw Robin Gurdon. We will follow him now and return to my G.1 later.

Travelling northward along the main Garawla track which goes from Mersa Matruh to Siwa, G.2 paused and inspected a conspicuous feature near the track which it was decided to use as a future rendezvous. Some of the trucks suffered mechanical trouble and had to be left under the Patrol's fitter for repair, while the rest pushed on. It was necessary to reach the top of the escarpment above Fuka aerodrome before dark so that Stirling's party could reconnoitre it before attacking it at midnight. This was done, though Gurdon had only two trucks by now. Stirling's party was intact. After dark Stirling went off with his men to the aerodrome, while Gurdon took his trucks down the track to the main road. They had some difficulty in passing a minefield and skirted an enemy vehicle park near Fuka station. At the main road they turned left and drove along it to the railway crossing. Having completed this reconnaissance drive, the party waited until 1.30 am, the hour when, as had been decided, they would start offensive action. Hardly any transport was using the road at night.

At zero hour Robin proceeded to shoot up the old NAAFI canteen, the tented camp near it and a tanker parked nearby, attacking them at point-blank range with machine guns firing. The vehicle park by the side was also raided. Here one of our trucks fell into a slit trench and had to be towed out. After this the party withdrew across country and drove south towards the rendezvous for the rest of the night. They fortunately stopped shortly after dawn and were therefore not seen by six enemy aircraft searching the ground in pairs. Later in the day they reached the rendezvous, where the remainder of the Patrol were awaiting them. Stirling's party, after raiding the aerodrome, were attacked by aircraft when approaching the R/V next morning and suffered some casualties in vehicles; this also happened to another SAS party and to Y.2 Patrol.

The position of the R/V was now considered compromised and at dawn next morning the whole force moved to a new one slightly further inland. This remained the base for further operations for several weeks. G.2 Patrol's wireless truck acted as "control" station for Stirling, whenever he was there, which was seldom. Another Patrol, T.2, under Nick Wilder, was due to arrive, and watch had to be kept for him at Tartura, further south, by parties of G.2 and Y.2 Patrols. Aircraft were now thoroughly stung into activity. A small enemy ground force had been seen and chased off. It was dangerous to travel in daylight, but this had to be risked for the sake of accurate navigation and because of the broken country which had to be traversed before reaching the open country near the coast.

Nothing happened for two days as far as G.2 were concerned, but on the afternoon of 11 July the Patrol set off with four of their six trucks to pilot two SAS parties with a 3-ton lorry to two landing grounds between Fuka and Daba. The parachutists were to be dropped two miles from each on the evening of the following day, while Robin, with two of his trucks, would again raid the main road, this time between Fuka and Daba. That night they halted at the old R/V and continued again before dawn in order to cover as much ground as possible before the

115

sun rose, with ever-imminent aircraft. After a while they halted in fair cover and lay up until 3pm, when they had to continue in order to reach the objective by dusk. At 5pm they met a long dune of sand which marked the northern limit of the hills. Robin's truck passed through a gap in this and halted in the open plain beyond. The rest of the trucks then filtered through and took up their stations, well dispersed.

At this point three enemy fighters, Macchis, were seen approaching from the west. They circled round, clearing their guns, and then attacked, paying no heed to Robin's attempt to fob them off by standing up and waving to them. Our gunners at first returned the fire, but they were then ordered to dismount some of the guns and take cover.

The two leading trucks were very much in the open. Robin's truck would not start, so he went over to the second one while the crew of his own truck took cover. As they started to move off a Macchi came straight for them from the front. Beside Robin, in the front seat, was Murray, the driver. Sergeant Stocker, navigator, and Corporal Wilson, gunner and medical orderly, were behind. Robin received two cannon shells just above the stomach and a bullet in the lungs. He managed to run a short way from the truck. Murray was severely wounded in the arm and was removed to a safer distance. The others were unhurt, though the truck started to burn fiercely. Corporal Wilson and Guardsman Vaughan, Robin's soldier servant, attended the Patrol commander as best they could, and others helped Murray. After a while some morphia was found and given to both the wounded, though the burning truck contained the bulk of medical stores.

After three-quarters of an hour the aircraft flew off, having failed to cause any further casualties. Robin remained lucid all the while, and he was consulted as to whether the party should go on to attack the landing grounds fifteen miles away. He replied in the affirmative, but his advice was not followed, and it was decided to try to get him back to the R/V. They travelled all through the night, but were much delayed next morning through the difficulties of navigating in the early morning fog. Robin apparently knew everything that was happening until near the end. He died at noon, four miles from the R/V. The Medical Officer was fetched from there, too late to do anything now, and he could doubtless have done little in any case. And

116

so Robin was buried there among the dry limestone hills far inland from the sea. He had hated the war, and the war had hated him and so many others of the best, whom it laid low.

Soon afterwards G.2 Patrol was ordered back to a new base where Group Headquarters had established themselves outside the Fayoum oasis, forty-five miles south-west of Cairo. They carried Murray with them. He took a long time to recover and was eventually evacuated home to England.

In the meantime G.1 Patrol under my command had gone off to Sidi Barrani from our SAS – LRDG (three Patrols) headquarters near Tartura. We had with us two SAS parties under Captains Warr and Schott, also their 3-tonner and jeep. The 3-tonner was a white elephant, or, to be accurate, a yellow one. While our own trucks had vindicated my choice of paint when refitting last March, this bulky creature was just the thing to attract every aircraft from miles around. The jeep, however, became popular. One of the SAS officers bashed its sump against a rock and then drove it until the oil had all leaked through a large crack, and then the engine seized up. We had been envious of the SAS for their jeeps for quite a while. The sight of so many at our first rendezvous was like a large sweet shop to a child. We took this one on tow and we doggedly took it with us wherever we went, finally all the five hundred miles back to Cairo where a new engine gave it a new lease of life, in the service of the LRDG.

After dropping both parties at their respective landing grounds in the dark, just east of the ruined village of Sidi Barrani near the main road, we lay up in a wadi near Sofafi. A Junkers 87 searched each wadi systematically all day, but luckily missed out the lower half of our own. That night I picked up Schott's party and also two of our own men whom I had left to watch a former water-point. But Warr's party was not at its appointed R/V. That night we travelled well inland. The area where we had lain up the previous day comprised the only broken ground in the neighbourhood, though there were plenty of maddening small hummocks for the last ten miles to the coastal road. So we crossed the railway, after an hour's sleep before dawn, and camped for the next three days in a small hollow in the open country of the south. Every evening we set forth, about two hours before sunset, to try to find the missing party, driving and searching all night long. On the fourth night we found them;

they had lost their way in this featureless country, but natives had looked after them. Their landing ground was much used in daylight but not at night, so they, too, had nothing to attack. By this time Sergeant Fraser was very ill with jaundice and I sent him back with two trucks to the distant main R/V of Stirling's, whence he was eventually taken back to Cairo.

Corporal Leach, chief navigator, in a bad way with dysentery, would not leave. Orders were now received to raid the main road before returning home.

An attempt to reach the road near Buq Buq failed. The going was extremely bad and when darkness fell it was impossible to go on. I decided therefore to try another point on the road nearer Matruh. We moved further east, noticing on the way fresh tracks along the railway line, and made a new camp well to the south where we left the 3-tonner and some of the SAS with orders to wait for us for at least two days. We again struck some difficult going when approaching the main road and the raid was put off until the following night. Next day we lay up near the water pipelines which used to serve the British forces when they were west of Matruh. I went back with two trucks to the rear party to warn them that we had postponed our raid and also to obtain water from our reserves, as we ourselves had almost none left. Unfortunately they mistook me for the enemy and made off at high speed towards the south, finally joining another LRDG patrol.

The water situation now appeared serious. I decided to inspect the old pipelines in the forlorn hope that they might have a dribble of water left. On loosening one of the couplings water spurted forth with the pressure of a natural geyser. We therefore filled our water containers and went on towards the main road. We waited here for some time after dark, but no vehicles passed down it and we saw no sign of the enemy. Unfortunately we had reached it rather late, after our trucks had fallen into several old slit trenches and gun pits of previous campaigns. Two days before, I had received by wireless the news of the disaster that had befallen G.2 Patrol, but I withheld the information from my Patrol for a time.

We had already received orders to proceed to Fayoum (where our new base was to be) at once, so we set off towards the south-east, blowing up the water pipeline on the way. We drove for a hundred miles along the familiar Matruh-Siwa track which led to our home no longer, and then broke off it, calling at Qara. I stopped to visit the Sheikh there to infuse into him what I could of morale. Then home across the Qattara Depression, arriving at Fayoum forty-five miles south-west of Cairo on 21 July, several days after G.2 had returned without their commander and his wounded driver.

Chapter Seven

DEADLOCK AT THE GATES TO EGYPT

In July 1942 8th Army, defeated but still in business, was established on the Alamein Line, its flanks anchored by the Qattara Depression to the South and by the Mediterranean on the north. A series of engagements followed against the advancing but now exhausted German/Italian army. Eventually the fighting petered out and both sides entrenched themselves behind minefields, in preparation for the decisive battle which one day must be fought. New generals, Alexander and Montgomery, arrived to command the "brave but baffled" 8th Army.

In this phase the LRDG were asked to assist the SAS in, and to undertake themselves, major raiding operations on Rommel's long line of communications. These operations on the whole were not successful, although the LRDG did have a success at Barce.

We had finally established an HQ at Fayoum, a large oasis group within easy reach of Cairo. The Patrol had as their quarters here some stone bungalows which had formerly served the Egyptian Police. They stood just next to the road where it dips down into the low-lying cultivated ground which comprises numerous oases, villages and the great lake, surrounding the main township of Fayoum. From our camp site, extending up the hillside, we could look down on these green fields and palm trees. Though pleasing to look on they would not have been as salutary to live in as the clean, dry rocks and gravel where we laid out our sleeping bags and pitched our little tents. A white flagpole was placed next to my tent. The flag was about 3ft x 2ft in size and was hoisted every evening when I was there and lowered at dusk. I had it made by Mohammed John, the tailor at Kasr-el-Nil Barracks. It had the Brigade of Guards blue, red, blue colours with a yellow scorpion in the centre. A miniature version was made which was placed on the left-hand mudguard of my jeep (a Divisional Commander's rectangular flag would be in the centre). I was much touched later when looking at my jeep from a stretcher, at the time of the dune accident when Wann and I were damaged; the little flag had been neatly folded around the staff.

Fayoum was healthier than Siwa and pleasantly close to Cairo, in fact one hour's jeep ride away, as was frequently proved. Yet we missed Siwa and I, for my part, looked back to the little house by the aerodrome there which Robin and I had shared in comfort. And again I had the experience of having lost the other officer in "G" Patrol. Some of the remnants of the Coldstream battalion were at this moment near Mena outside Cairo. I went off to see them at once to ask for another Patrol commander. It was first suggested to send Michael Brodrick and then finally Ken Sweeting, who joined us a few days later.

The whole of "G" Patrol meanwhile had three days' much-needed special leave in Cairo and Alexandria. Everyone could now clean up and look smart. In fact there was not a man who did not take a pride in doing so as a contrast to the scruffy appearance we inevitably presented when on operations. Those who had forage caps or khaki drill would dig them out of the Citadel, and the streets of Cairo would see guardsmen looking much as they had done in 1940.

While we were at Fayoum we took part in several football matches at the Fayoum Sporting Club, an Egyptian organization where this sport and others were enthusiastically supported. Having seldom more than one or two Patrols at base at the same time, LRDG teams were not of high standard. Our star player, however, was undoubtedly my soldier servant, Thomas Wann, with whose excellence I was always proud to be associated, and I would go like every other fan to watch him play. The very fact that our forwards and halves were often unable to keep the ball far from our own goal provided all the more opportunity for Wann to display his massive acrobatics, and so far as the score went at least we never suffered an ignominious defeat.

Two other companions of ours did not survive the summer.

121

G.1 Patrol, when searching the previous May for Waiting and Astell, had found a cheetah's lair. It was a blunder by those in that search party and I was very angry at the time. The cave they found was empty except for three tiny cheetah cubs. The large paw marks of their parents could be seen all around. Two cubs were removed, leaving one. When I saw them I said that they must be taken back. But we were still desperately searching for Waiting and Astell and it was getting late. No one quite remembered the way to the cave, so I had to keep them. All the way back to Siwa they made little squeals from the locker behind my head in which they were kept. Cheetahs in Libya must be very rare. I cannot imagine where they found enough water, forty miles inland from the coast. The two cubs had been carried with us back to Siwa, then to Alamein, and finally to Fayoum. Their diet had not been ideal, for concentrated tinned milk was all we could give them. One of them had never been healthy and eventually died at the end of July. The other, however, was robust and lively and had grown up fast in our care. One day in August he disappeared at Fayoum. In Siwa no doubt this would not have happened, but here we were too near the so-called civilized part of the Middle East.

Meanwhile, the two battalions of the Coldstream and Scots Guards, which had been operating as one composite battalion since the battles on the Gazala Line, were eventually withdrawn from operations on the Alamein Line. I visited my own regiment near Amiriya near Alexandria and the Coldstream at Mustafa Barracks, Alexandria. We required some new men again and these eventually arrived.

G.1 and I had only been back a week when we were sent out again. David Stirling's forces were still operating in relays behind the Alamein Line and we were required to join them. We had just reached a point near Qara on the far edge of the Qattara Depression when David decided to return home and we were recalled. We expected to find Qara occupied by the enemy, since Siwa had been taken a fortnight before. We entered it with the idea of doing some damage, but discovered that the enemy had only sent along some armoured cars which he had then withdrawn. We received, during this trip, all kinds of information by wireless regarding large enemy forces which were supposed to be operating in the Qattara Depression, but we found none.

I did, however, meet an interesting little unit on that trip. It comprised about ten Egyptian soldiers with a young officer. They were mounted in two well-equipped Ford trucks, quite unlike our Ford 30-cwts. as they had windscreens (which none of our vehicles ever had) and were less loaded with jerricans, water cans, piles of camouflage nets and strips of cloth. They were doing a patrol from the Farafra oasis in the undulating sand and gravel south of the Qattara Depression. The soldiers looked quite alert. The young officer spoke good French and we had a long talk. He was not supposed to go further west, but he begged me to let him come with me. I said that we were liable to meet enemy troops and Egypt was technically neutral. He persisted for a long time as he wanted to have a crack at the enemy which had invaded his country in 1940. His enthusiasm for doing something in the war and his delight in desert travel has always remained for me a repudiation of the common idea among British troops that the Egyptian army was not much good.

In the middle of August G.1 Patrol had ten days' leave. After this all of us felt much improved in general health. Most people lost their desert sores at least for a time, though the rot had eaten deep into some people, especially Sergeant Stocker, who from now on suffered from increasing poisonous growths in one leg. But then he had been with LRDG in desert operations for two years.

One evening I was dining in Cairo at the Embassy. I was sitting on the left of Lady Lampson, the Ambassador Sir Miles' wife. On her right sat a Brigadier who suddenly, towards the end of dinner, leant across our hostess and said, "Can you come and see me tomorrow". I thought Oh! God! Have I been indiscreet and said something taboo? I had, I thought, been in rather good form. The conversation had ranged informally over stimulating topics. The Brigadier said nothing more to me after dinner except to give me his name and address and I said I would drive in from Fayoum the next day. He was one of the chiefs in Military Intelligence and he had with him in his office a Colonel Astley who was in charge of publicity at Middle East Headquarters. What they wanted me for was not to tell me to keep my mouth shut, but to open it wider. German propaganda was plugging the line that Britain was fighting almost exclusively with colonial troops – Indians, New Zealanders, South Africans and Australians – as well as Poles, Free French, Czechs and

Greeks. Military Intelligence was getting seriously worried about the success of this propaganda. As a counter-offensive for us, what could be better than the commander of the Guards Patrol of the Long Range Desert Group? He represented something really British and had an exciting name. Would I do a broadcast?

I naturally said that it was not the sort of thing to appeal to a unit which was trying to be as clandestine as possible. The Germans were very confused about our operations, which was just what we needed, and they mixed us up with other organizations such as the SAS and various commandos or ex-commandos. Anyway, I would put the question to my commanding officer, since they were very insistent.

The upshot was that Guy Prendergast, my Commanding Officer, summed up our discussion by saying, "You, not I, must be the judge. If you Patrol commanders get into trouble through publicity, you will be the most direct victims." I talked it over with Jake Easonsmith and I decided to do something as helpful as I could without saying anything which we presumed they must know or guess, and even some misleading remarks. My text, a copy of which I have still, is incredibly dull, full of vague expressions: our emphasis was on "vigilance", operating almost anywhere with complete surprise, but keeping to the Geneva Convention as regards the treatment of prisoners and the injured, as far as we could.

A few days later Richard Dimbleby (the father of Jonathan and David) took me in charge. He gave me lunch and we passed a pleasant afternoon together. Richard Dimbleby at that time ran BBC News Broadcasting. He had to keep up a stream of over-optimistic statements about how well our forces were doing: "Rommel's defeated troops are now withdrawing hastily westwards, harassed by the Royal Air Force". We could listen to this sort of thing on the 9.00pm News from London within hours of us watching German and Italian soldiers singing and cheerful as they camped or moved along the main coastal road.

When we arrived at Broadcasting House that evening Richard went through the formality of handing my script to the censor, who stood inside a little window at the doorway leading to the room where I was to broadcast. He just handed it back. Standing around were American and other journalists of allied countries with stop watches rehearsing their scripts and checking their timing. One of them rushed up with a text. "Here is an urgent item," he said to the chief engineer. "It is from General de Gaulle". "That will have to wait," was the reply. "We have Captain Timpson of the Long Range Desert Group here." So on I went with Richard Dimbleby and an assistant. They sat in chairs by the wall opposite me. I was at a small table next to the side wall. The room was large and the walls were sound-proofed with green baize. The chief engineer sat at the little table opposite me and quite close. A microphone stood on the table between us. He pointed to a clock above us, fixed to the side wall. The minute hand was moving round and a red light was showing. "When the minute hand reaches the top of the dial," he said, "the red light will turn to green and I shall point my finger at you. You will then be on the air for six minutes."

I had practised the timing of my piece during the afternoon. It sounded more boring every time I read it. As the clock had moved up I felt very nervous. I would be speaking to thousands all over the world. Would I be putting my companions in jeopardy? What would enemy information technologists make of some enigmatic remark? I could imagine not only enemies – Germans, Italians and Japanese – but also allies and neutrals, all listening in (Phoebe, my wife, had been alerted, but heard indistinctly). I read slowly the words which were becoming an abomination, pretending some excitement in relating my duties as a Patrol commander. I only just kept myself calm enough to get through. Richard Dimbleby said it was "excellent". He was probably being as inaccurate as he was obliged to be with his news broadcasts. I imagined my listeners thought so too.

During this time at Fayoum until 1 September new operations for the Patrol were contemplated. John Haselden was again backing a forward policy. We thought seriously of making a raid on Siwa, the geography of which we knew so well, in the same way as we had considered attacking Jalo the previous April, and, as happened then, nothing came of it. The plan which John Haselden eventually formed and carried out was the foundation of a far more ambitious scheme which will be described in the next chapter.

In the meantime G.2 Patrol, now commanded by Ken Sweeting, after interchanging some of its personnel with G.1, left for an operation. In company with Y.2 Patrol under Hunter, it went as far as the beginning of Cyrenaica with additional

125

petrol to enable Y.2 to cover the distance to the Benghazi area and the Jebel Akhdar – now seven hundred and fifty miles from Kufra. Here Y.2 picked up some ISLD personnel and Major Peniakoff's party, and with G.2 Patrol returned to Kufra. Major Peniakoff had been operating in the thickly inhabited area of the hills for several months, having provided by wireless information about enemy movements as well as having made a few raids. I got on well with Popski in those days, though he was a swashbuckling figure and not to be taken seriously, but he later took against all the Brigade of Guards type of officers.

This was the last occasion on which it was possible to pass through the Qattara Depression and Qara, for the enemy occupied the area in strength immediately afterwards, thus rendering the task of passing to the rear of the enemy lines very difficult other than by Kufra. Ken Sweeting, with G.2, reached Kufra on 20 August and finally got back to Fayoum, after travelling by way of the Gilf Kebir and the Nile valley, on 29 August. They took ten days' leave. Then G.1 and I set forth on 1 September, a small part of the force which was to spread out from our bases at Fayoum and Kufra to help with large-scale expeditions to attack Benghazi and Tobruk, apart from an LRDG target of our own – Barce.

By August the Alamein line was stabilized, and both sides were preparing to attack the other. In order to assist and exploit an intended offensive by 8th Army, proposals were put forward for disrupting the enemy's ports and lines of communication in the north of Cyrenaica, far behind the enemy lines, to coincide with a limited offensive by 8th Army on the Alamein Line.

The plan emanated from Middle East Headquarters. When they got instructions to abandon raids close behind the front lines, David Stirling and his officers were angry. They had just accomplished the highly successful 12-jeep raid on Landing Ground 12 near Fuka, and were ready to pounce again from hide-outs between the escarpments, which lay to the south of the coastal plain and north of the Qattara Depression. Stirling then had under his command over a hundred men – SAS, a Free French party, two LRDG Patrols, signallers, mechanics and transport personnel. A Bombay aircraft landed on a bit of flat ground at night and took off with David Stirling and some wounded men. It would have been better if the authorities in

Cairo had left him to continue with the raids he was doing already, and planning for more, on Egyptian territory close to the enemy's over-stretched front.

The proposals were ambitious and grew even more so with the formulation of operations planning. Colonel John Haselden (now up-graded two ranks after being appointed G(1) Intelligence, Cyrenaica – thoroughly deserved, as anyone reading about my road-watch party with him six months earlier will agree) would lead a 100-man Commando to attack Tobruk and its harbour, starting from Kufra as a base about 750 miles to the south (after completing the preliminary journey from Cairo to Kufra of 750 miles now that it was impossible to enter Cyrenaica unobserved by way of the western end of the Qattara Depression). The Royal Navy would attack at the same time from the sea, with a much larger force, starting from Alexandria, 300 miles east. It would include Royal Marines and naval personnel who would land at the harbour as soon as Haselden's force had seized the coastal guns and given the code word. After destroying all installations our forces would withdraw. The date set for the operation was the evening of 13 September 1942. The Commando would withdraw to Kufra after it had done its work.

On the same date Stirling's SAS was to attack Benghazi with a force of about two hundred and fifty men, eighty jeeps and thirty 3-tonners. They were to destroy harbour installations, shipping, aircraft on the neighbouring landing grounds and storage tanks. Stirling's force would also use Kufra as its base on the outward journey, and would have much the same distance to cover to reach its objective. On its return from Benghazi it would make Jalo its main base and not go on south to Kufra.

By this time David Stirling had got over his initial resentment at being frustrated in his raids close behind the enemy lines. This ambitious plan appealed to his exuberance. Before the various parties left their starting points it was learnt that the enemy had obtained information about our intentions. 8th Army postponed its offensive, so the operation became no more than a large-scale raid and did not conform directly with the tactical issues which concerned our main forces. It was hoped that the raids would at least so weaken the enemy that any attack he contemplated would miscarry.

The enterprise had originated when Auchinleck commanded

8th Army (as well as being GOC-in-C Middle East). The new generals who took his place, Alexander and Montgomery, were very sceptical when they arrived and cancelled the offensive at Alamein for the time being. The LRDG modestly suggested that they might also be of use and were prepared to carry out tasks both independent of the other two forces and in conjunction with them. And finally the Sudan Defence Force would be glad of an opportunity to take part in offensive action and thereby break the monotony of their garrison duties at Kufra.

The tank procured by the SAS, which was included in Stirling's equipment, did not get far on its way to the starting line at Kufra, let alone Benghazi, but it had a significance, like Monty's cap badges. The significance, however, denoted very different mentalities. Audacity was David's driving force, but he had no personal vanity, except to exceed, if possible, the score of his subordinate, Paddy Mayne, in the destruction of enemy aircraft, ships and all forms of transport and installations, and so end the war in Africa quickly. It may also be true that David's two personal visits to Benghazi harbour and the SAS's havoc at nearby landing grounds gave him a sensation of invincibility when taking on the ancient capital city of Queen Berenice and now the main operational base of Field Marshal Rommel. It is difficult to explain the calculations behind the attacks on Benghazi or Tobruk, once security was known to be compromised, without resort to fanciful speculation.

Anyway, the plan went ahead. The SDF, starting from Kufra, would attack the oases and villages comprising Jalo (300 miles north) in order to secure a future base of operations for the SAS,and to safeguard the withdrawal from Benghazi once that operation was completed. Two LRDG patrols would accompany this force. Another two of our patrols would accompany the SAS in its attack on Benghazi. David Lloyd Owen, with Y.1 Patrol, would go with John Haselden to Tobruk. The only party consisting solely of LRDG personnel was a small force of two Patrols which was due to attack Derna aerodrome, this target being subsequently changed in the last week to Barce, its important landing ground, railway station and barracks. It would start from Fayoum and include G.1 Patrol under my command. It is with this force that we are now concerned.

Our route from Fayoum to Barce was both long and difficult. The distance was 950 miles and involved crossing the Great

Sand Sea between Ain Dalla and Big Cairn, that is from east to west, at right angles to the line of the large dune formations; and later crossing it again further north-west by the Garet Khod route. As we had only 30-cwt trucks and jeeps such a route was feasible, whereas the large number of vehicles leaving Kufra would consist partly of 3-tonners and even a tank which David Stirling hoped to urge all the way from Cairo to Kufra and then northward as far as it would go. Moreover the forces leaving Kufra would have to pass close to Jalo, held by the enemy, and it was desired to relieve the congestion of traffic in this narrow corridor.

The maximum distance a 30-cwt can travel, carrying its own petrol, is about 1500 miles, while a jeep can be self-supporting for only 900, if fitted with an extra tank. Therefore two Mack 10-tonner lorries accompanied us for the first 250 miles from Fayoum to Ain Dalla, near the beginning of the sand sea, where we re-fuelled. A second supply of petrol would be waiting for us five days later on the far side of the sand sea where a detachment of our Heavy Section would meet us from Kufra. After refuelling there the force must continue to Barce and withdraw to Kufra on what it could carry itself.

The force was under the command of Jake Easonsmith, now second-in-command of the LRDG. The centre of communications would be Fayoum, with wireless link between there and the operations room in Alexandria, where our Commanding Officer would be when the offensive started. Besides G.1 Patrol, T.2 Patrol (New Zealand) under Nick Wilder was also to attack Barce. The Medical Officer came with us, and also Major Peniakoff with two men of the Libyan Arab Force. S.2 Patrol (Rhodesian) under John Olivey came with us as far as Big Cairn, but was later detached to join Stirling's force in the Benghazi area.

Before going further I want to say a word or two about Jake Easonsmith, who was one of those who most influenced me during my time with the LRDG. David Stirling always said Jake was our best Patrol commander: he and David Lloyd Owen had picked up the survivors of "L" Detachment SAS after their abortive attacks on the enemy landing grounds at the opening of the Sidi Rezegh battle. Lloyd Owen has said that there was nothing like Easonsmith's calm and authoritative manner in making everyone under his command confident and cheerful, notably the rugged New Zealanders in his Patrol. This quiet English wine merchant, with his calm and kindly judgement, went on to command the LRDG and was killed at Leros in the Aegean trying to repel the German attack on that island.

Before reaching the sand sea we skirted the oases of Baharia and Farafra and stopped briefly at Ain Dalla for water from the spring and petrol from the 10-tonners. Beyond this began the long lines of dunes stretching right across our route. They came out of the north in long white barriers, towering into razor-backs 300 feet high at times and mostly sharp at their crests, and so stretching away endlessly south. The distance between the crest of one range and that of the next was about a mile. To start with they were not very high and fairly smooth. To start with, the black gravel still showed in the troughs between, but after surmounting the first four or five dune barriers one is in a world of nothing but sand. Whoever is in the lead takes what he thinks is the best line where the sand is hard and keeps going as fast as he can so as to charge through the soft patches that he is bound to meet. When the leader sticks the following trucks try to pass to the left or right, as they think best, to avoid the soft patch where the leader has floundered, and wait near the top of the next ridge on a hard patch of sand. On this trip each Patrol had to keep together, but the order in which the Patrols marched varied as each became marooned in a soft patch of sand. We all knew where we were going and we generally met in the evening. A Patrol which was in the rear nearly always caught up a Patrol in the front by following its tracks until they found the pioneers deep in their temporary graves, when they would take up the lead and try to seek a more successful route onwards.

The side from which we approached each line of dunes was normally the steep side, the east side, whilst the western side from the crest undulated gently to the trough below the next steep formation. One had to travel north or south near the crest, often for a long distance, to find a "col" between the high, steep sections of the next range. We would then go for the col at top speed, hoping to avoid the softer patches or plunge through them if they were small enough, hoping to remain at a good speed until one could relax on top of the col. One would then look westwards at the next range and wait for one's Patrol to re-assemble. If in the lead, I would not wait for the other Patrols,

130

but continue with an attempt at the next range. The other two Patrol commanders and Jake Easonsmith and his HQ would do the same. Hard and soft patches were difficult to distinguish, by colour or any other guesswork. Some of my men would compliment me after a long run without floundering, but adding that I was "not as good as Major Clayton". Pat Clayton had been head of Egyptian Desert Surveys, an early explorer, wounded and captured in the first attack on Kufra in February 1941 with the Free French from the Chad.

On the morning of the sixth day after leaving Fayoum, when we were in the lead, I drove my jeep with Wann next to me over a twenty-foot drop. It was a freak col. Had I known that this was the last range, the most westerly of the Great Sand Sea, I might have been more wary. Wann was very seriously injured, his spine being broken. I had a slightly fractured skull. I clambered back to the top of the razor-back and the rest of the Patrol stopped just in time. We were now nearly at the end of the sand sea. Wann and I were carried on the backs of two of our trucks with awnings spread over us until we reached the gravel country of Big Cairn. The presence of the Medical Officer undoubtedly saved Wann's life. After two days a Hudson aircraft arrived from Kufra, navigated by Tony Browne (a former Patrol commander, then doing a job at Middle East Headquarters) and flew us back to Cairo and to a hospital. S.2 Patrol and the Doctor looked after us during most of this time. Then John Olivey and S.2 went on westwards to join Stirling near Benghazi, whilst Dick Lawson and his party of orderlies, etc. hurried after the other two Patrols and our Force Headquarters, who were pushing on northward to Barce.

They refuelled, crossed the next stretch of sand sea of about a hundred miles, the Garet Khod route, and eventually arrived near the foothills of the Jebel of northern Cyrenaica without incident. Here it was decided to hide one 30-cwt with sufficient petrol to get back to Kufra and a small quantity of water and rations as an "escape truck" in case of mishap. It was placed in a large patch of scrub near Bir Gerrari, well known to members of the party from previous trips. This was to be the rendezvous for any stragglers.

The attack on Barce was scheduled for the night of 13 September, the same as the Tobruk and Benghazi parties. That morning the force reached the foothills and Major Easonsmith took Peniakoff and the two Libyan Arabs who knew the region well to find out what they could of enemy dispositions and report to the force at a certain place near the main road leading into Barce that evening. One aircraft had been seen up till now, but had apparently taken no notice, and an hour before dark a number of reconnaissance aircraft could be seen combing the area for many miles around. The party was probably not seen as the light was bad and the camouflage good.

At dusk the force moved on, driving along a track that led from an enemy fort to the main road; the telephone wires were cut on the way, in case the force had been seen. Lights were not used until a police post was approached. Here an Italian native soldier was standing on the track and challenged the leading truck. Lights were switched on, he was dazzled, disarmed, placed on a truck and became from here onwards a useful guide. A shout for help was made on his behalf by a member of the party. This brought out an Italian officer who was shot. There were a number of buildings here by the side of the road; men were seen to run out of them. The trucks became somewhat involved among the buildings, backing out and turning round, with inhabitants peering out and hastily closing their windows. Grenades were thrown into the military post. One of the trucks was damaged. It was stripped of its gear and left close to the road. A mile further on a machine gun opened up but was soon stopped when we fired back at it. Near the main road Peniakoff was duly picked up, but his two Arabs had not yet returned. Here T.2 Patrol's wireless truck was left, as Stirling, commanding the force attacking Benghazi, had requested that a continuous wireless watch be kept that night for messages from him. The Doctor also was left here in charge of this kind of rear rallying point.

At 11pm the force moved on and reached the main Barce-Maraua road in good order. Here headlights were again switched on. At the top of the escarpment some five miles out of Barce two enemy light tanks were seen on either side of the road. They naturally could not be certain who we were and as the column passed them all our trucks opened fire, passing by them unscathed. The party next stopped at the main fork roads on the edge of the town and each Patrol went to its respective objective. T.2 Patrol drove off to deal with the aerodrome, while G.1 Patrol were to cut the telephone wires in the middle of the town and attack the railway station and the main barracks on the far side of the town, leaving their wireless truck at the cross-roads to keep watch for any pursuing vehicles, and generally to prevent attempts to block our withdrawal.

We will follow G.1 Patrol first, under the command of Sergeant Dennis. They dealt successfully with the telephone wires and then attacked the railway station. Here they found one locomotive, which was administered with time bombs, as was some rolling stock. They then went on to the enemy barracks, which occupied an extensive area on the far side of the town. Grenades were lobbed into the windows and every calibre of machine gun sprayed doors and windows. Such activities were cut short by the arrival of a tank. The Patrol had a lively time dodging round blocks of the barracks and other houses, while the tank responded only with machine guns. The Patrol became some-what split up, but the majority finally got away after the raid had lasted for two hours. They met, by perfect timing, T.2 Patrol and Major Easonsmith at the crossroads, as had been arranged. The Patrol had, however, lost one of the four 30-cwt trucks – Findlay's. Four men were missing.

T.2 Patrol under Nick Wilder meanwhile had carried out a most successful raid. They had driven on to the landing ground by the main entrance, after setting fire to a large petrol dump, and had driven round the aerodrome firing incendiary and tracer into the aircraft and placing bombs on those that were reluctant to burn. The enemy ground defence eventually retaliated and replied with heavy fire. Having destroyed or damaged thirty-two aircraft, the Patrol commander found the exit blocked by some light tanks which had arrived on the scene. Wilder drove his own truck full tilt against the flank of one of these and cleared a passage through the entrance by which his Patrol managed to escape, he and his crew ascending another vehicle, since their own was wrecked. The fire from the enemy tanks was inaccurate and so was that of another tank they met on the road outside. But, as we have seen, the majority of T.2 Patrol, after suffering some losses in vehicles and personnel, reached the crossroads on time.

Jake Easonsmith, the Commander of the force, had not been content to leave the work of destruction entirely to the two Patrols. He had been driving his jeep around the town, firing his double Vickers "K" at everything and everyone he saw and throwing grenades at various parties of soldiers he found in his way. He then found an enemy vehicle park consisting of ten vehicles and one tanker with trailer; these were left unserviceable after applying grenades and Tommy gun fire to them. He, too, was chased by enemy tanks, eluding them eventually to reach the crossroads and lead the whole party back up the road. The way leading out of the town was found to be clear. The two light tanks originally seen guarding it had moved away; in fact they could be heard making their way across country towards the aerodrome. At the top of the escarpment the party reformed and looked back on the town now lit up in a blaze of light from the burning dumps and aircraft on the landing ground and other fires resulting from the raid.

On the way back to the MO at the rear rallying point one of G.1 Patrol's trucks overturned and some time was taken in righting it again. Dick Lawson, the MO, attended to the wounded as best he could and the whole party pushed on south. The track in this area runs along the bottom of a valley. Shortly before reaching the military post passed on the outward journey a brisk fire was opened up by the enemy with rifles and machine guns. It later transpired that there were a hundred and fifty native soldiers under three Italian officers at this place. A bullet burst one of the tyres on Dick Lawson's truck and the crew changed the wheel in under three minutes, spurred on by some enemy fire. Dennis and Duncalfe circled round the 30-cwt in their jeep, blazing away with their twin Vickers "K" at wherever enemy fire came from. The truck which had been abandoned that evening was duly taken in tow, so that, with two other damaged trucks, there were now three 30-cwts on tow altogether. Beyond the military post, as dawn was breaking, the enemy fire increased and three men were wounded, but no material damage was inflicted on the vehicles. It was soon broad daylight and cover had to be found to repair the vehicles. About nine miles beyond the enemy post a wood of small trees was found. Here the party camouflaged their trucks and the fitters got to work. Two of the damaged trucks, it was considered, could be made serviceable, but one would have to be abandoned. Such administrative problems were soon superseded by some of a more pressing nature.

Native troops mounted in trucks came up, but quickly turned about on sighting our trucks. Then a party of about sixty native soldiers approached and started to fire on the party. A few minutes later two CR42 fighters began to fly around and the ground troops fired some smoke cartridges to attract the aircraft's attention, but fortunately failed to do so and the aircraft flew off. It was obviously highly desirable to move again. Jake then drove G.1 Patrol's jeep with Duncalfe as gunner in a sally against the enemy ground troops, going up behind them from the rear and shooting at them with a high volume of fire. The result of this action was most effective. The enemy withdrew a mile or two, enabling the whole party to move on again after removing the stores from the three damaged trucks and leaving time bombs in them. The party moved on another seven miles over very bad going. G.1 Patrol's wireless truck unfortunately broke down on the top of a very bare hill. The other vehicles found good cover among some trees at the base of it, but a reconnaissance aircraft came over at once and spotted the stranded truck. As soon as it left, the delinquent vehicle was pushed down into the deep wadi, but too late, for six fighters now arrived on the scene.

For a while the explosions of our time bombs in the vehicles abandoned further back attracted the enemy aircraft. They machine-gunned the burning trucks and then started to fire into other patches of cover close to the position where the party was. Eventually the aircraft found our trucks one by one, attacking them with incendiary and explosive ammunition and setting them on fire. The men removed some of their guns and took cover, for the most part, away from the trucks. All day long from now, about 10.30am, until dusk the enemy kept up their attacks in relays. The only 30-cwt which survived was that which contained six wounded men. Dick Lawson lay on the top of this truck at the height of one of the attacks in an effort to cover one badly wounded man who could not be taken to cover. Eventually this truck was moved during a slight pause to a safer place a mile away. As each truck was found and attacked Jake and Nick Wilder and others tried to unload it and remove its vital stores to another not yet discovered, but this work was all in vain. Every 30-cwt except the doctor's was destroyed. Nick Wilder was wounded. The last 30-cwt to be destroyed was T.2 Patrol's wireless truck, so that now the force's last means of communication was gone.

At dusk the only surviving 30-cwt set off with the MO, six

wounded, a navigator and a fitter, towards the rendezvous where the spare truck had been left to pick up some rations, and would thence make its own way to Landing Ground 125, far south of Trigh el Abd. Our Commanding Officer had arranged, with his usual foresight, to make this an emergency rendezvous for the whole operation in case things went badly. Lloyd Owen's Patrol, which had accompanied the Tobruk party, was still intact and was directed by Headquarters at Siwa to Landing Ground 125, as by that time no news had come from Easonsmith's party for two days. Here Lloyd Owen found Lawson and the wounded. After he had sent this news to Headquarters by wireless an aircraft was promptly sent out to bring the wounded back. They all survived.

Meanwhile Jake Easonsmith with the main party set out to walk towards the spare truck, eighty miles to the south. The only transport was one jeep, in which was kept water, some arms and ammunition and where the more exhausted occasionally took a ride. The party had started to walk at different times and was therefore split up, so that several groups of men were lost, including Duncalfe and McNabola. No one had much water, but some were fortunate enough to find an old well on the way southwards. Help arrived for several of the party in the form of S.2 Patrol under John Olivey. They had been directed by Headquarters in Siwa to search this area for our survivors, having done all they could to help with the SAS's unsuccessful assault on Benghazi. The majority of those not found by S.2 Patrol eventually reached the spare truck and drove it to Landing Ground 125. Jake himself stayed behind in the area for some days, walking about a hundred and fifty miles in search of stragglers. Eventually Y.1 and S.2 Patrols found nearly everyone and took them back to Kufra. Except for Corporal Findlay, McNabola, Duncalfe and Head, the personnel of G.1 Patrol reached Kufra on 25 September.

Duncalfe and McNabola spent the next two months leading the life of Bedouin until they were finally picked up by the advance of 8th Army after the battle of Alamein. Corporal Findlay was found by a party of ISLD under Captain Grandguillot, (an officer of Belgian nationality who commanded a force of friendly Senussi Arabs) who handed him over to G.2 Patrol a fortnight later.

After experiencing a fairly stiff air raid at Kufra, G.1 Patrol left for Cairo to find new trucks and equipment. In spite of our heavy casualties in vehicles, the Barce raid was a success. The attacks at Tobruk and Benghazi and Jalo, on the other hand, were failures. John Haselden's force seized the coastal guns at Tobruk, but was driven off them as the Navy started to land. John himself was killed while leading a counter-attack. David Stirling's attack on Benghazi was met by enemy forewarned and fully prepared. Most of their 3-tonners, half of their jeeps and many of their men never returned. The Sudan Defence Force company which attacked Jalo in order to secure the return route of the Benghazi and Tobruk parties met with more vigorous defence than expected and never secured the main village and fort.

The results of this grand design were, on balance, very negative. One lesson was clear: surprise was paramount for an attack by small forces against an enemy with large potential reserves. When security is compromised the attack must inevitably fail. The solely LRDG force which attacked Barce was alone successful, and it was the only one whose objective had been changed at the eleventh hour.

I recovered fairly quickly from my injuries, caused by my own incautious driving, and returned to duty on 10 October 1942. My soldier-servant Thomas Wann was not so lucky.

Chapter Eight

VICTORY AT ALAMEIN

The Battle of Alamein, fought in the last week of October 1942, was a hard slogging-match and ended in the defeat and retreat of Rommel's German/Italian army. Pursuit was inhibited by heavy rain, by the caution of General Montgomery and by the near-exhaustion of 8th Army formations.

The LRDG's functions from now on were, first, to maintain their all-important roadwatch; secondly, to harass the retreating enemy. From now on they were to be concerned with Tripolitania, which was a long way away from their main base at Kufra.

The Battle of Alamein opened on 23 October 1942. On 31 August Rommel had made his expected attack on the Line. At the Battle of Alam Halfa he had broken through near the southern end and attempted to sweep round behind 8th Army to Amiriya and Alexandria with his main forces, while a flying column would go straight for Wadi Natrun and down the main road to Cairo. The offensive, however, was beaten off. Never again was the Afrika Korps and the Italian Libyan Army to attack towards the eastern horizon in the hope of seeing the palm trees of the Nile. From now on they had to look over their shoulder to their rear, to their line of withdrawal and their next defensive position: first Alamein then El Agheila, Buerat, Tripoli, Mareth, Akarit and finally Enfidaville near Tunis. Each one of these might provide the breakwater against which the on-rushing force of 8th Army would spend itself and recoil, as they themselves had done at Alam Halfa and Alamein, and, a year before, at Sidi Rezegh.

That each of these obstacles was surmounted by the Middle East Forces, including operations by land, sea and air with the help of the Free French from the Chad, appears from the story of their success as the inevitable dispensation of destiny. Yet this was not so. Every impediment in the advance westwards was broken by hard fighting. The enemy was not making unduly optimistic calculations, even after Alamein and the landing in Algeria, in assuming he could retain part of Africa and still eventually regain the whole.

As we have seen in the last chapter, the LRDG was employed, shortly before the great battle, in concerted raids in Cyrenaica. After Alamein the rapid advance of our forces in the north precluded extensive use of the LRDG and SAS in eastern Libya, and both units were mostly concerned during this phase with Tripolitania. Group Headquarters and all available Patrols were concentrated at Kufra. So Siwa and the Fayoum were no longer needed. The SAS, now much expanded from new reinforcements, likewise used Kufra as their base. The LRDG was allotted chiefly long-range reconnaissance tasks. These included carrying ISLD and G(R) agents far to the west, and a few parties to the Cyrenaica Jebel just ahead of 8th Army. On 23 October, the first day of the Alamein battle, the road-watch at Marble Arch, after a break of three months, was started again. Both G.1 and G.2 Patrols carried out their share in these operations.

G.2 Patrol, with Ken Sweeting, spent ten days' leave in the Nile Delta while G.1 were occupied in the raid on Barce, and then returned to Kufra. They spent some time there awaiting further orders. Rain hardly ever falls there, and huts made out of palm leaves were as good as bricks and cement for protection, and infinitely cooler.

On the last day of September G.2 set forth for northern Cyrenaica. They were to take a party of ISLD and others to the Jebel, contact Grandguillot's party already there and search for surviviors of the Barce raid. Just before entering the Sand Sea by the Garet Khod route Guardsman Crossley, chief navigator, became very ill. An aeroplane flew out to fetch him and bring up Sergeant Stocker, now attached to Headquarters, to take his place. Nothing startling occurred during the trip. Some difficulty was experienced in finding Captain Grandguillot, who, when found, decided to come with the Patrol back to Kufra. A large number of derelict trucks of the SAS were inspected where they had tried to hide near Benghazi after their raid and had been heavily strafed from the air. None of these trucks, however, could be made serviceable. Findlay was picked up, as mentioned previously. After successfully carrying out their tasks the Patrol therefore turned home, reaching Kufra on 16 October 1942. Here they stayed until their next trip on 10 November, the last week being spent in the company of my G.1 Patrol which arrived from Cairo on 3 November to start work again.

Of G.1, Wann and Murray, both severely injured with me in the Great Sand Sea accident described in the last chapter, were lying in the 15th (Scottish) General Hospital before being evacuated home. I myself spent two weeks in this excellent hospital. Visitors always entered one's room with a pre-arranged smile. For the first few days it would have been better if mine had been less well-intentioned. It was distressing to see their expression change to one of horror. When both eyes were half-closed and what was open was red, surrounded by bruises and bandages, there was not much one could do except to apologize, and to assure them that underneath I was better than I looked. But I was very soon in good shape and colour and went off on sick leave to the delights of staying with the family of Zaki Wissa Bey at Sidi Bishr on the sea at the eastern edge of Alexandria.

Wann, however, was in a very bad way. Twice the surgeons stretched his body. The second operation lasted five hours. Still they could not make his spine get back into the right place and his spinal cord function. A friend, Elizabeth Oldfield, was a nurse at the 15th Scottish. She used to come down to my room to report on Wann every day. It was amazing, she said, how Wann would remain cheerful and cheering up everyone else in his ward, even though he was in a worse state than most of them. He was eventually sent home by sea. Phoebe, my wife, visited him in hospital when he got back and much later, in 1945, I could do so too, at Musselborough Hospital outside Edinburgh or at Easton House. This was part of an establishment called the Thistle Foundation paid for by Michael Crichton Stuart. Wann was married to Maizie, the sister of one of my men in "G" Company, which I commanded in Tunisia and later in Italy. Thomas and Maizie lived at Easton House and I saw them there when I could. They adopted a boy as they could not have children. Thomas got well enough eventually to have a small car which he could drive with his hands only. He drove me around Edinburgh in it once, but his driving was more fortunate than

140

mine. The last recollection I shall relate is when at Easton House, Edinburgh, I had given Thomas the year before a silver cigarette case. It had the LRDG badge, a scorpion, on one side and the Scots Guards badge on the other. He opened the case and offered me a cigarette. After taking one, I said to him, "I always feel dreadful about my responsibility for what happened to you." He replied, "You should not worry, Sir. I never regret having gone with you to the LRDG."

Lieutenant the Hon Bernard Bruce arrived from 13th Corps Headquarters to join "G" Patrol, with a view to taking over command from me when he had had some experience in the job. I would then return to my battalion.

Replacements for Scots Guards other ranks were found, but the 3rd Coldstream could not manage reinforcements, so the required number was made up by 6th Battalion Grenadier Guards. This battalion had recently arrived in the Middle East to join the Guards Brigade, now in Syria, and sent one officer, 2/Lieutenant Anthony Kinsman, along with seven other ranks. Up till now "G" Patrol had been inevitably limited to Coldstream and Scots Guards personnel; we were glad to feel more representative of the Brigade of Guards by reason of this contingent of the 1st Foot Guards. Thus we soon had three officers (in addition to Ken Sweeting still with G.2 at Kufra) and a full complement of other ranks. Sergeant Fraser became Patrol Sergeant of G.1 instead of Sergeant Dennis, who left. So far as manpower went, we were now well up to scratch. New transport and equipment, however, took longer to obtain.

There were no more 30-cwt Canadian Chevrolets left. A ship carrying a new supply had been sunk en route to the Middle East and we had been obliged for some months to reduce the number of vehicles held by Headquarters and the Patrols to conserve our last reserves. No other alternative remained but to resuscitate the old 30-cwt Fords which we had cast aside as unserviceable on a patch of sand by Tel-el-Kebir the previous spring. REME guaranteed their revival in accordance with a prescription that only they knew. All our drivers knew was that they would not go when the time came for them to take their place at the steering wheel and sign all the bits of paper which army workshops required when selling something they are glad to be rid of. The trouble was they could not be rid of them. It is unfair to say that the Fords would not go at all. Two out of our

G.2 Patrol five trucks reached a point several miles along the Cairo road from Tel-el-Kebir before breaking down. The New Zealanders of T.2 Patrol took their own fitter and several spare parts with them and succeeded in driving one of their trucks all the forty miles to Abbassia. Faulty workmanship was ascribed to the more unskilled among the Egyptian workmen at the Tel-el-Kebir workshops, and perhaps this was understandable since it was now the month of Ramadan, during which period Muslims take no food or drink from sunrise until sunset; their performance suffers progressively. The observance of their religious duties haunted us for long afterwards, and the curse of the Prophet seemed to follow our trucks on our way to Kufra and far off in Tripolitania.

Two jeeps were also given us, loyal friends as jeeps always are. My own was a worthy successor to my previous one lost at Barce, and the patrol flag was hoisted on it again. It was a marvel of reliability in our next operation. All trucks were at last persuaded to reach Abbassia. The steering assembly on one was rectified by screwing it on the right way. In appearance at least they were no worse than when discarded last March. Then the complications of gunnery were tackled and finally solved. Small and large aircraft Brownings and Vickers "K" formed the basis of fire power. Signal and navigation equipment was fitted. A novel camouflage device was adopted: lengths of hessian were sewed into enormous canopies by Mohammed John, the tailor at Kasr-el-Nil Barracks, and then sprayed with pink and green paint. Stocks of "goodies" and some drink were laid in, though the NAAFIs of the Delta were no longer so well stocked as they used to be. The Patrol set off for Kufra on 26 October while the early stages of the battle at Alamein were still in progress.

We had with us Captain Mark Pilkington (Life Guards) as guest. We had known each other for many years, so I was very pleased to have him for company in my jeep as far as Kufra and, we hoped, to come with me on my next patrol. He had been sent by Glubb's Arab Legion, together with seven of his men, to be attached to the LRDG for a while. They were dressed in military uniforms, service dress or battle dress, but wore on their heads the red and white Arab Legion keffiehs. Mark wore his khaki service dress cap with Life Guards badge. At the time it could not be assumed that 8th Army would advance as rapidly as it did; in fact it might not advance at all. Opportunities might therefore occur for using the Arab Legion in western Libya. So Mark was to come with us to Kufra and beyond to see what Glubb could do to help. Mark had spent thirteen months in guerrilla warfare in Abyssinia, before joining Glubb's Legion, the best trained force in the Arab World. So he was not new to this sort of job.

The whole party of about fifty men was housed and entertained for one night at the home of the Wissa family at Assiut on the upper Nile, two hundred and twenty-five miles south of Cairo where our route turned off into the desert. The trucks gave considerable trouble, showing that their old appetite for oil had not diminished much as a result of their rest. On reaching Kufra, which was done in slow time, they were given an overhaul at our own workshops. Here G.1 and G.2 met up again. But the duties of the road-watch at Marble Arch soon called out each Patrol in turn.

On reaching Kufra we heard of the great victory at Alamein, and how the enemy were now withdrawing across the frontier of Egypt. As the enemy recoiled westwards, the road-watch was now of increased importance. Soon he could no longer use the ports of Cyrenaica for his supplies and depended solely on his communications with Tripolitania, all of which passed before our observers' eyes. His base units were the first to shift back and these caused much difficulty to the LRDG watch party by camping in large numbers nearby. The aerodrome at Marble Arch, defunct for some time, now came into lively use again. This still might not have been so bad, but the enemy was kept in a state of angry unrest by the raids of the SAS now operating in small parties along the coastal road.

Before dealing with G.2 Patrol's trip to the main road, a word first about Mark Pilkington's only trip with LRDG. It was hoped, when we reached Kufra, that he would be able to stay with me and G.1 Patrol for our next operation. Mark and I and Billy McLean had shared a flat in Cairo a few months earlier and it now seemed a good idea to share a truck. The life of a Patrol commander is a trifle lonely. Although I now had Bernard Bruce for company, why not make it quite a party? Colonel Guy Prendergast decided, however, that it would be best for Mark to go with R.1 Patrol, New Zealanders, under Tony Browne, to take some spies far west, to the area south of Misurata, a thousand miles away. It had bigger distance to cover than my next (and last) operation, but it was expected to be more predictable.

They left Kufra on 11 November. On climbing the escarpment between Marada and Zella they exchanged shots with an enemy force, but suffered no casualties and went on. Refuelling at a dump made by our Heavy Section, known as Deniff's Dump, they were later spotted by enemy aircraft when crossing the open country near the coast. They tried to hide up by the cliffs of Wadi Tamet, but several attacks by enemy fighters were made. Just after midday fourteen Italian CR42s made a determined attack and were little affected by the fire put up by the patrol. They mortally wounded Mark and the Patrol navigator, who both died soon afterwards. "Both men were shot," states Captain Browne's report, "while firing machine guns."

G.2 Patrol, under Ken Sweeting with Anthony Kinsman, left Kufra on 10 November. On the way to Marble Arch they were informed by HQ in Kufra that the Patrol then on road-watch had been chased out of its position by enemy forces and Sweeting was therefore to find and establish a new look-out with all speed in the area between Merduma and Nofilia, further west.

They had difficulty in finding a safe hiding place for the trucks and a look-out. Several enemy camps were installed in wadis near the road. Eventually continuous watch by two men was started on 19 November at a point ten miles from their camp and trucks. Two 30-cwts were used every evening to change reliefs. Native camps were also numerous. As their inmates were not friendly, they were a continuous source of anxiety. Ken also found that it was difficult to find one's way in this region, an experience shared by G.1 Patrol later. Inland was flat hard gravel and scrub, with small hollows. Beside the road were some low hills and fairly deep wadis, but they were all exactly alike in appearance. The close presence of enemy camps forced one to move about chiefly in the dark, and this was no aid to navigation, either on foot or mounted.

On 27 November, eight days after the watch started, the Patrol was due to be relieved by either G.1 or T.2 Patrols starting from Kufra, 650 miles away. Unfortunately the wireless set was not working satisfactorily and also the Patrol commander was not feeling his best, for Ken had contracted jaundice. He decided to leave at 11 pm, two hours, as it turned out, before G.1 and I arrived at the vacant camp site. The following night the Patrol eventually contacted headquarters by wireless, but by then had travelled some way inland, and they were ordered back to Kufra. They succeeded in avoiding enemy forces patrolling the Marada-Zella gap and reached base on 7 December, having been away four weeks – a week longer than the period for which their rations were scheduled. Ken Sweeting was evacuated to Cairo, while his Patrol stayed with Group Headquarters at Kufra, which soon started to move north and west, in order to be within better reach of the Patrols operating further west as the main forces of 8th Army advanced into Tripolitania.

Chapter Nine

AT THE END

At the beginning of the 1942–3 winter 8th Army had pursued Rommel across Cyrenaica and was preparing its final push on Tripoli. The LRDG kept up its road-watch on the main Via Balbia, information about the retreating enemy being of vital importance. This task was more difficult in Tripolitania, owing to the hostility of the local natives and the large numbers of enemy camping near the road.

Alastair Timpson's last operation, before he returned to his Battalion, was full of incident and "G" Patrol suffered serious losses, but the job was well done.

On 20 November G.1 Patrol under my command left Kufra, ten days after G.2, to relieve the latter on road-watch in the Nofilia-Merduma area. By this time 8th Army had taken Benghazi and Agedabia and was coming up against the enemy defensive position on the El Agheila-Marada line. As the enemy proceeded to concentrate in this defended area he was in a better position to detail some of his forces to guard his southern flank, now more limited in extent and geographically favoured by escarpments where the mountains faced the sandy plains of the south. For the last few weeks our Patrols had encountered enemy forces and mines on entering the "back-door" of the Marada-Zella gap. In addition, therefore, to the usual worry of enemy aircraft we now had to contend with opposition from the ground before reaching our objectives behind the enemy lines in Tripolitania.

The importance of maintaining the road-watch, now only a hundred miles behind the enemy's front, was so vital that two Patrols simultaneously were despatched from Kufra in order to make certain that the operation would not fail. Thus, T.2 Patrol

146

left at the same time as G.1. Each Patrol travelled by slightly different routes as the Patrol commanders determined. My Patrol was larger than usual: five 30-cwt Fords, two jeeps, twenty other ranks, Bernard Bruce and myself. We had nearly all the new recruits, Scots Guards and Grenadiers, besides a fair sprinkling of old hands like Sergeant Fraser, Lance Corporal Leach, chief navigator Lance-Corporal Inwood, Guardsmen Knight, Wheatley, Blaney and Anderson, and Wheeldon (Royal Corps of Signals). One of the jeeps was mine, and driven by me as usual. The other jeep was Sergeant Fraser's.

We ran into unusually bad weather on reaching the first line of escarpments in the Marada-Zella gap. This was welcome so far as aircraft were concerned, but on the night of the 23rd, when we camped on top of the final abrupt ridge, we could make no astrofix. This was particularly inopportune as we knew the enemy patrols in this area were using a dominating height called Hofra as their base. We were attempting to pass west of it, but the formation of the escarpments forced us to approach it very close. Our camp that night was probably within a few miles of this danger-spot, as far as we could tell by dead reckoning. As the grey clouds overhead grew paler with dawn we moved on, following the edge of the escarpment which was forcing us unpleasantly close to Hofra. It was drizzling slightly. After two hours we sighted a line of vehicles ahead of us, halted in extended order from the edge of the escarpment and away to the right. The vehicles were facing us, about a mile away; I counted eight. Some of them appeared to be armoured cars. They had about six to eight men in each. As my orders were to reach the road, I must avoid a fight if possible.

I doubled back, keeping behind a low ridge, intending to turn up north-east after half a mile. As I did this another enemy force with six vehicles was seen approaching. It had apparently been watching us and had come up behind us from the high ground of Hofra. I then swung left, to pass between the two enemy forces. We had been manoeuvring on a stretch of ground where the top of the escarpment made a kind of "peninsula". The party which had come up behind us was trying to close the eastern side of the peninsula and now the force we had first sighted was moving fast, closing in on the western side and joining up with the others. In doing so they left a gap behind them near the escarpment. I wanted to drive for this gap, but had to wait. A

147

truck in the rear was having mechanical trouble, so the other trucks had halted. Desultory fire had been going on for some minutes. I drove my jeep into a hull-down position behind a bank and Wheatley started to blaze away with his double Vickers "K" at the left-hand enemy trucks, which were those directly in front of us. Bernard Bruce, driving the next truck, halted on my right and his guns got into action, and the next, Sergeant Ollerenshaw's, did the same. The remaining trucks came up and took up positions on the right, but were badly bunched on rather high exposed ground. The escarpment was immediately behind us, dropping almost sheer for 150 feet to the plain below. Every time I drove out of my firing position in an attempt to visit the rest of the Patrol the enemy trucks opposite us would take the opportunity of our reduced fire to move further to our left in order to close the gap between them and the escarpment. On one of these attempts I visited most of the trucks and warned them to be ready to move on. The firing went on for about fifteen minutes with the enemy growing closer, particularly on the right. The enemy fire was directed chiefly at the right of our line where the trucks presented the best target. Some mortar fire and heavy calibre weapons also were giving our men here some trouble. Our Breda gun truck appeared to be hit fairly heavily and most machine guns had been dismounted from the exposed gun mountings and were being fired from the ground. Guardsman Hannah on No. 4 truck, a new member, was doing good work firing his Vickers "K" from the top of his truck. When it jammed he took over another 0.5" water-cooled Vickers behind the driver's seat. The truck was then seen to have a bad knock from a round of the larger enemy gun. I made a rapid trip round the Patrol, for the enemy were slowly closing in. I shouted to all to get back into their trucks and be ready to follow me in a break-out. Then, returning to left of the line and giving some last long bursts with our machine gun, I drove over the bank and made to pass left of the enemy trucks. Only two 30-cwt trucks followed me out. Bernard Bruce's and Sergeant Ollerenshaw's. Three 30-cwts and Sergeant Fraser's jeep did not.

We passed the enemy's flank and four of their vehicles started to follow us. The two old Fords went faster than I believed possible. While bumping along we exchanged shots with the enemy at fairly close range, but gradually we pulled away from them. One by one they dropped out. Two chased us for about ten miles. We had to try to lose our tracks as we went, so I followed various old enemy tracks, turning off them abruptly in a wadi bed and then dodging this way and that behind small hills. We halted as soon as we lost sight of the enemy in the hope of seeing some more of my Patrol following, but no more came. We zig-zagged further for another ten miles, repeatedly changing direction on hard rocky ground, until I decided it would be best to hide up for the rest of the day in a small wadi, since we must expect to see enemy aircraft looking for us soon. No aircraft, however, showed up, though some were heard. I sent a message to Headquarters stating briefly what had happened and that I would continue to the road-watch with what I still had: two 30-cwts, including the wireless truck, one jeep, two officers, one signaller (Wheeldon) and seven other ranks, Ollerenshaw, Leach, Blaney, Wheatley, Welsh, Anderson and Ferguson, ten in all. There was little hope of going back at night to look for the rest of the Patrol. The enemy had fourteen trucks and they were rapidly closing in when we left. The escarpment made retreat impossible. Headquarters informed us, moreover, that the other Patrol sent out with us, T.2, had suffered casualties in a minefield and had turned back. G.2 Patrol, due to be still on road-watch, had not been heard for some days and might be in trouble. We must therefore reach the road and keep the watch there going.

That night again the clouds never broke to show us some stars for an astrofix. We moved on northwards at about 2 am. During the next day we made vain attempts to obtain our position by the sun. As a result of two cloudy nights and days our navigation was now very unreliable, and yet accuracy was essential in order to locate G.2 at their camp by the road, assuming they were still there. One aircraft passed over without spotting us. The next night was again cloudy, but the following morning we reached some country I knew from a previous trip and obtained our correct position from our old camp site near to where we had buried Guardsman Matthews last May. We were due to take over from G.2 that evening.

At 10 pm that night we reached the wadi next to their camp, but we spent several hours in finding the latter which was now deserted. (They had moved off at 11 pm as I found out later.) I presumed that G.2 would be still maintaining a watch on the road and had changed the position of their camp, though there was a possibility that they had run into trouble and had been chased off by the enemy. At dawn I followed their tracks ten miles to the south, and then came back and lay up for the rest of the day in order to find out from Headquarters by wireless what G.2 were doing. There was a good deal of aircraft activity, for we were just between the Merduma and Nofilia landing grounds, now among the enemy's main fighter and fighter-bomber bases. We could hear their aircrafts' engines revving up at both aerodromes, particularly at dawn. I had not noticed in the half-light that our hide-out was only 300 yards from the inland track between Merduma and Nofilia, and we had a bad moment when a small enemy convoy drove slowly by. Our trucks were pretending to be part of some sparse bushes, the only ones in this open featureless area, and Wheeldon was noisily tapping out a message to Kufra with the poles of the Wyndham aerial hoisted high. But they never noticed us.

We could not contact Headquarters that day, but finally got through at midnight, after following G.2's tracks for twenty miles southwards. We were informed they were another thirty-five miles further south, so at dawn I drove on in the jeep, only to find their camp site there had just been evacuated. This attempt to contact G.2 had already cost one and a half days' delay. It was essential to re-establish the road-watch at once, so I returned to my two 30-cwts and moved on northwards. These two trucks were in somewhat unreliable condition. The big end bearing on one was sounding an unwelcome warning and the steering of the other was unsound. We had petrol for 550 miles, not enough to reach Taiserbo, let alone Kufra, water and rations for three weeks, but these did not include any sugar, tea, ciga-rettes, oatmeal, and only a little milk, all of which were kept on the lost cooker truck. We were expected to maintain the road-watch for ten days. In actual fact we eventually had to do so for fourteen. As the inland track was being used it was advisable to establish our camp just south of it, a distance of about thirteen miles from the coastal road. We therefore moved to Garet Areica, which was nearer to Nofilia and away from the area where G.2 might have run into trouble, for all we knew. We found, however, no cover there.

I went on after moonrise by jeep to establish the first look-out on the road with Guardsman Welsh, taking Corporal Leach and

Wheatley as navigator and driver. We halted at a point four miles from the road after passing various native camps. Here Welsh and I continued on foot while the other two men returned with the jeep to rejoin the others. Bernard Bruce would then try to find a place with reasonable cover as a camp site for all three vehicles, not more than ten miles south of Garet Areica, about twenty six miles from the coast road. At dusk the next day the jeep would take the next watch party to Garet Areica, whence they would walk about sixteen miles to the road, to be in a position on watch at midnight. At this hour the first watch party, Welsh and myself, would leave the road and walk back to the rendezvous at Garet Areica and return in the jeep to the camp chosen by Bernard. It was not feasible for successive reliefs to take over the same look-out as it would be unwise for one party to try to locate another in the dark in close proximity to the enemy, when both would be trying to elude discovery. The distance to walk was considerable, yet at first I thought it expedient, in order to avoid making numerous vehicle tracks across the inland road which passing enemy might notice and trace. Welsh and I walked close by a few dormant enemy parked in a wadi near the road. The hill above them was bare and rocky, and here we constructed a low "sangar" of stones from which we could well observe the road 400 yards away below us.

At dawn the traffic started and was fairly heavy throughout the day. There were a few enemy camped in the wadis below our hill on either side and some behind us. But they were not many, nothing like the number which flowed off the road on later days, as 8th Army pressed the enemy back from their positions near El Agheila. We were too busy, also, in watching the road to pay much attention to what happened to the vehicles which pulled off it. Some tankers at sea passed going east close inshore, and we longed to call up the RAF by wireless, for they were deep in the water. If this continued to occur it might be possible to hide up our wireless truck close to the look-out and lay on some long-distance target observation.

It drizzled that night. We sat close to the road in the dark, glad to be able to stretch our limbs and eat some food. Very little traffic passed after 8 pm. At midnight we left. By one hour before dawn we had walked about seventeen miles and should be close to Garet Areica, a feature marked on the map, but not in the least prominent on the ground. We lay down for an hour waiting for

151

dawn. We heard the jeep start up close by, and it nearly ran me down in the dark. At dusk it had not been certain of the rendezvous, and was now looking for it. It swerved on seeing me in the half-light but did not stop, thinking I was a native, and drove off southward. No doubt I was a bit scruffy. When the razor and the bath tub are dispensed with perhaps there is not much difference between any prototype of Western and Middle Eastern civilization. I assumed it had just left the rendezvous and was making for the camp, presumably not more than ten miles to the south, for some unknown reason. It seemed we would have to walk on, following its tracks.

After covering a mile, we came on one of the numerous native camps which stretched far inland in this area. We now had no water left and were very thirsty and tired, for we carried a fairly heavy load: waterproof greatcoats, grenades, rifle, tommy gun and ammunition. The Bedouin were suspicious of us. They sat around us in a half-circle and asked us threateningly if we were British. On assuring them we were Germans, they became less menacing, but our dishevelled appearance was not calculated to arouse respect.

In my bad Arabic and their Tripolitanian dialect, very different to the homely chatter of the Senussi of Cyrenaica, we discoursed on the close friendship between the Arab and the German races, and our common dislike of the Italian. This latter at least was a genuine sentiment. I thought fit, however, to enlighten them as to the course of the campaign. It was indeed going very badly for us Germans. Benghazi and Agedabia had fallen; they did not know this, and were astonished. El Agheila, too, had just been entered by the hated British. This was not true at the time, but was received with much clicking of tongues in sympathy. They might easily guess we were British, in spite of our denials at the start, so I thought it prudent to enhance British prestige. They asked what type of weapon my tommy gun was. It was a Schmeisser. My water bottle they considered very small for a litre. They wanted to inspect the tommy gun, but I held onto it firmly. Then they asked me to fire it. I declined as gracefully as I could, for I knew it was much too dirty to function. If they knew this they might well set on us. Where were we going? To Nofilia. We had just come back from the front, and my truck was due to pick me up here, having lost me in the dark. At least I was not giving the Germans credit for much competence. Why not get a lift on one of those German trucks which one could see passing down the Merduma-Nofilia track a mile away? An awkward and reasonable suggestion which was not very satisfactorily answered. At last, however, they brought bowlsful of goat and sheep's milk. They could spare no water. We drank it as slowly and in as nonchalant a manner as possible. The somewhat undignified durbar was brought to an end by a jeep appearing on the horizon, careering along at high speed, circling round us, but never stopping for long enough for us to catch it. We waved and shouted, but it disappeared again. Leaving Welsh to follow some of the jeep's many tracks in this area, I set off southward to try to find our camp. After walking thus for ten miles, I turned back, for I still had no water. It was noon and very hot. Perhaps the Patrol had run into trouble and had gone far inland. Welsh and I might be able to steal a German truck near the coastal road. But we must find water soon.

I came back to Welsh near Garet Areica. I had two shirts and pawned one of these with the natives for some more milk and some home-made Arab "esch", a kind of bread. They were not likely to read the Jermyn Street address on the collar. This kept us going while we waited until dusk. At last Bernard Bruce arrived driving the jeep with Anderson. We drank our fill of water. Unfortunately no one had any cigarettes. The lack of these was really worse than that of sugar and tea during the next thirteen days and nights. We all drove on at once northward to the road. I decided that each watch party must be taken much closer to the road by jeep in future, so we drove to within three miles of it, dropping Bernard and Guardsman Anderson as next watch party. The point where I dropped them would be the rendezvous for the next night and all future nights. Welsh and I slept by the jeep here until dawn and then drove south to the camp, whose location Bernard explained to me, since I had not seen it yet. This was well chosen, at the bottom of a small wadi in a low escarpment facing south. The ground was covered with hard stones on approaching it, so that, by zig-zagging on these, our tracks would not easily be followed. Had I continued one mile further on my walk the previous day I would have found the camp. On arrival here I made out an analysis of the traffic seen on the road and sent it by wireless to Kufra. Activity on the road was obviously increasing and its details, together with estimates of troops seen and unit signs observed, had urgent news-value which warranted immediate transmission to Headquarters. The danger of being D/F-ed was a very minor risk, and we invariably sent back every day an account of the previous day's road-watch. The procedure from now on was that the jeep left camp every afternoon at 4 pm with the next pair for the watch, together with a driver and one other man, four in all. It would halt at the R/V three miles from the road and about twenty-two miles from camp, and from here, after some cold supper and a short rest, the new relief of two men would go off on foot, to be in position by the road at 11 pm. The other two who stayed with the jeep would await the returning watch party who must remain on look-out until midnight – a 25-hour watch. Thus, an overlap in time of one hour between successive reliefs ensured continuity. This was important, for gradually the amount of traffic at night increased. Having completed the relief, the jeep would return to camp at dawn.

The country near the R/V was rough, with small sand hummocks, and some deep wadis close to the R/V itself. There were also two native camps nearby with their patches of cultivated land. It was therefore difficult to drive around here in the dark. On one occasion we became embarrassingly involved in one of the native camps in the dark, running over some tent ropes and arousing loud remonstrance from the inmates' dogs. We retired before listening to what their owners had to say.

So we duly reached camp next morning, and that evening I acted as driver again, taking Sergeant Ollerenshaw and Guardsman Blaney as next relief, with Corporal Leach as company. When close to the R/V we noticed a man a few hundred yards off shouting and waving to us, but he could not be seen clearly against the setting sun. We stopped and he came running towards us. It might be Bernard (for he had a map in his hand), having met trouble while on road-watch. As he came close we saw that he was a hatless enemy officer, probably Italian. I shouted to him in German to ask what the matter was. We had passed an Italian aeroplane that had landed, presumably with engine trouble, near Garet Areica, and here was its pilot who took us for Germans and wanted a lift to the road. Should we bump him off? Or take him prisoner? I suppose this unknown Italian will never know how his fate hung in the balance. It was not kindness that spared him. If we took either of these alternatives he would obviously be missed by somebody and a search made for him in this area, which was quite lively enough already. So I drove slowly off, waving to him. In truth we were full up in the jeep; he had only two miles to walk to the nearest enemy camp and such small lack of consideration as we showed was doubtless common between the two partners of the Axis. We left our acquaintance yelling and swearing. One more drop of discord was added to the ruffled waters of German-Italian friendship.

To guide the incoming watch party to the R/V it was arranged to flash a torch from the top of a small hill every fifteen minutes starting at 1.am: three flashes was the challenge, and two the answer. That night, however, Bernard and Anderson came in by perfect navigation at 1 am without any flashing of torches. Nor was it necessary to have recourse to another device: starting the engine of the jeep, a unique noise to those familiar with such excellent creatures, and revving it up every few minutes. Both visual and audible signs were therefore used to pilot tired home-comers to the R/V. These expedients were not in the least superfluous. The exact rendezvous was usually difficult to find both by the jeep party at dusk and the incoming watch at night. The jeep party had to cross the inland track on both outward and inward journeys, and would pass at times within full view of the traffic on it, and had also to pass close by the native camps near the R/V. And all the while aircraft flew fairly frequently over-head. It was therefore advisable to approach the R/V as near dusk as possible, and leave it at first light. Our navigation was thus rendered inaccurate at times by travelling in darkness. An incoming relief on foot was liable to make errors in compass marching. The country, even near the road, contained no unique features, but ones of a repetitive size and shape. When enemy camps started to sprout and spread, the watch party had to make detours or double back trying to find a suitable look-out position by the road at night, or when leaving it on the following night at the end of their twenty-five hours' watch. So they too were apt to miss the R/V.

The fourth night of this road-watch was a difficult one in this respect. Bernard Bruce took the relief party, Corporal Leach and Guardsman Wheatley, in the jeep on this occasion. After flashing torches and running the jeep's engine, Sergeant Ollerenshaw and Blaney finally found the R/V, but not until dawn, after prolonged use of both piloting devices. The watch party had run into a new and large enemy camp in a wadi by the road the previous night, but walked away unseen, and were in position by the road only an hour late; so there was no break in continuity. On the fifth day Guardsman Wilson and myself provided the next watch party; Bernard Bruce and Anderson again on the seventh; Sergeant Ollerenshaw and Blaney on the eighth night. A heavy deluge of rain came on and when I drove back to camp, having duly picked up Bernard and Anderson, we found that the downpour had rushed down the small wadi and caused much inconvenience to the four men with the trucks, soaking the bedding and kits of all of us, which were kept beneath the camouflaged trucks. From the sixth day on, rain fell frequently. One felt cold at night when on watch after lying motionless in the rain all day.

During the eighth and ninth days enemy reconnaissance aircraft searched the ground near our camp. They kept trying to follow our tracks and some old ones not made by us, but never found us. They may have been searching for us or for other Patrols, especially those taking part in the SAS's new offensive tactic of repeatedly raiding the Via Balbia between Sirte and Tripoli. It might also be the result of reports from numerous natives who saw us pass them every day at dawn and dusk. Or the enemy might have heard our wireless set by D/F.

But more worrying was Bernard Bruce's sudden illness. He developed blood poisoning and a temperature of 103.5°. We treated him with sulphanilamide, and Wheeldon, the signaller and only permanent camp-dweller among us, looked after him as best he could. Wheeldon was always a cheering and reliable companion. He and I would work all day helping to summarize the voluminous results of the previous road-watch party, then encode it and finally transmit it. The last phase alone would often take three or four hours. He also did much to cheer those returning tired to camp. At the start we had a tin or two of treacle and also of Nescafé. A portion of these luxuries would be the prerogative of the incoming relief, prepared by Wheeldon for our return after dawn. He never had anything but bully beef, biscuits and water himself. Later on, that was all anyone had.

With Bernard out of it, we were now eight, in addition to Wheeldon. Up till now six of us out of nine had to be out all night, including the pair on watch. Those who could navigate or drive the jeep had disproportionately less rest. Those who had an aptitude for mathematics were kept busy when at camp making a summary of the previous day's traffic and encoding it. With the traffic ever increasing, particularly westbound, this job and the final transmission would take nearly all day. The four at camp, moreover, took turns as sentry, both day and night. I therefore decided to send the jeep out each night with a driver only in addition to the reliefs. This meant a lonely vigil for the driver between dropping the new relief at 9 pm and picking up the incoming pair in the early hours of the morning, but it reduced those out all night to five.

On the seventh night I dropped Corporals Leach and Wheatley and picked up Sergeant Ollerenshaw and Blaney; on the eighth Welsh and I were dropped by Sergeant Ollerenshaw alone; on the ninth Corporal Leach dropped Anderson and Wilson and picked Welsh and me up with much difficulty after dawn. The tenth night I dropped Sergeant Ollerenshaw and Blaney, but there was no sign of Wilson and Anderson, due back before dawn. At 3 am and 5 am I let off some Very lights, in addition to constant torch-flashing and running the jeep's engine. I stayed at the R/V for an hour after dawn. It was a bright sunny morning and one could plainly see the tents and vehicles of an enemy camp a mile away. I drove slowly around for several hours, stopping at the top of surrounding hills, and went for some way in the direction of their presumed route to the road. After pausing beside two native camps, in case they had called in there to obtain nourishment, as Welsh and I had done on the first day, I followed our vehicle tracks slowly home. They might have missed the R/V and started to walk the twenty-two miles to camp.

I reached camp about midday. There was no sign of Anderson and Wilson. We were now reduced to six, beside Wheeldon, but not quite as black as sweeps, for I had ordered road-watch parties to shave. I considered that our normally bearded and scruffy appearance might attract attention among such enemy as were liable to see us when approaching or leaving our look-out post by the road. We were, moreover, rather tired by now, and it would be difficult to go on much longer at this rate. It was now 11 December and we had started our watch on the night 29/30 November. Shaving made one feel better generally. With all this rain, water was not a problem.

Headquarters was meanwhile doing all it could. Two more

Patrols had been sent out from Kufra to take on the road-watch, but at a point further west, since our area was being over-run by the retreating enemy forces, who were clearly pulling out of their defensive position near El Agheila. (Traffic was now 2,000 westbound vehicles a day, besides some eastbound. On our last day, 13 December, the westbound figure reached 3,500.) In addition, Indian Patrol No.1, of the Indian Long Range Squadron now attached to the LRDG, was on its way north under Lieutenant Cantley to bring us help in the form of rations, petrol, spare parts, a fitter to administer to our lame Fords and a medical orderly to attend to Bernard Bruce. Their personnel were, however, not trained to record enemy equipment with accuracy and would not be able to carry out road-watch duties. All these patrols were much delayed by the difficulties of a new route further west which had been opened up between Zella and Hon, to avoid the dangers of the Marada-Zella gap. None therefore had reached the coast by 11 December. We must hold on until one of the two Patrols to our west had established a new watch on the road.

After some lunch, to continue our story, I left camp again at 2.30pm with the next relief, Corporals Leach and Wheatley. We left at this early hour in order to search the R/V area for the missing men before it grew dark, but we could not find them. They were not, in fact, seen again until two and a half years later when they returned as ex-prisoners of war. They had been discovered in their hiding place near the road when the enemy formed a new camp around them, but managed, first, to jettison any incriminating papers, in particular their record of the day's traffic. I dropped Leach and Wheatley and picked up Ollerenshaw and Blaney. It poured with rain. Before returning to camp I again searched the R/V for an hour after dawn for Anderson and Wilson. We expected Cantley with Indian No.1 Patrol to arrive that day, but he did not come. Nor were our hopes fulfilled of hearing that a Patrol had established a watch further west. Sergeant Ollerenshaw dropped Welsh and me that evening and picked up Corporal Leach and Wheatley later. The only space near the road unoccupied by the enemy was a wadi with steep sides, but flattening out close to the road where the shallow bed contained a few thorn bushes. These were not very thick and rather short, but grew on small hummocks which gave good observation on to the road. During the night we sat in one of these, by the road's edge, and moved back to one 200 yards from the road at dawn.

Traffic was heavy throughout the night, nearly all driving west, and at first light it grew even thicker. And then they started to pull off the road. In the first truck came the German camp commandant. He liked the look of the ground on the right of our bush and proceeded to allot the area to each lorry as it drew off the road. They halted all around us and drove up the wadi behind us, but luckily none were parked immediately between us and the road which we could still observe clearly. We crawled gingerly from one side of our bush to the other as a party of Germans came up to our hide-out and decided it was an excellent place for their cooker-lorry. "*Sie koennen ruhig hineinfahren,*" ("you can drive in all right") said the man who guided the truck into position. They halted just short of our bush. Of the other lorries about six were within 100 yards of us and scores within 200 yards. Our chief worry was that they would think of using the dry thornwood as fuel for their fires. There were only about eight thorn bushes like ours, and no other natural fuel was available. It did not seem very hopeful that we would see the day through undetected. Automatically we continued with our traffic census. "West. Three 3-tonners; German. Covered, many troops in back", Welsh would whisper ceaselessly, while I would write. The density grew so heavy that one could not write fast enough and it was only possible to keep the record going by quickly making a list every ten minutes of the different classifications of vehicles, troops, stores, equipment and unit signals, and adding a mark against each type as it passed, in the manner of scoring at cricket. After a while Welsh would take over the score and I would observe and whisper.

And so it went on all day. Men walking between trucks would come unpleasantly close. We only heard German spoken. Our neighbours were well disciplined and cheerful. We could have assured the BBC that the retreating Afrika Korps was not in the least a "shattered remnant". Even the Italians, who were crowded all over many of the passing lorries, sang lustily of Napoli. At 12.30pm the German party next to our bush had macaroni, goulash and gherkins for lunch. We heard the menu described, we could smell it being cooked, but we could not taste it. Nor could we move to reach our own tins of bully left on the other side of the bush. The repertoire of songs included chiefly somewhat outdated American jazz numbers, but such music held little charm for us. Nor did it seem the moment to raise our own spirits with a duet in "Land of Hope and Glory", let alone "Rule Britannia". Levity in retrospect of such incidents is easy, but things were earnest enough at the time.

The twelve hours of daylight gradually drew to a close. A number of Germans were sitting round the cooker lorry, gossiping about Sergeant this and Captain that, and ragging one another, much as our soldiers do. An armed sentry stood nearby. The moon was shining at intervals between the drifting clouds, which brought occasional showers of rain. A British Beaufighter roared over at 8.pm strafing our area and the traffic on the road which was still moving densely west. Five minutes later it came back and did the same. We saw nothing hit. The Germans took hasty cover in slit trenches, but soon reassembled, laughing. I wanted to leave before midnight to prevent the next relief from coming to this area. Up till now this was the only vacant stretch of ground that remained near the road. I knew they intended to make for it.

At 9 pm we gingerly started to pick up our belongings – rifle, tommy gun and magazines. The moon was still rising, but even when it was behind the clouds we could see, and be seen, for far around. It was no good crawling or sneaking away. We moved to the edge of the bush away from the cooker-lorry and towards the road. We then stood up briskly when I muttered, "Now". We at once walked off slowly, in a nonchalant way, first towards the road and then swung left in a semi-circle, in the hope of walking past the various parked vehicles and so continue inland. A German sentry challenged, demanding the password. We walked on slowly. He challenged again, in an excited voice. I replied, "Friend" in German, but this was not of the least use, for he fired a shot from 40 yards away and, as we continued to walk slowly past, he fired again and again. At this rate he would hit us soon, so we started to run. Numerous other voices all round swelled into a clamour; shots were popping off about us. The chase was on.

Our equipment and heavy coats did not ease the task of our legs, stiffened from inactivity all day. We crossed the open ground ahead of our pursuers and reached the deep part of the wadi, at the bottom of which flowed a torrent of water three feet deep. Here we paused to take breath. The Germans could move faster than us and some were now rushing past along the top of the river-banks, firing down into the wadi with rifles and automatics. We stumbled on through the water. I fell down in it several times and lost sight of Welsh. I then doubled up the side of the wadi, passing between two parties of pursuers, who nevertheless caught sight of me and gave chase. They were overhauling me, but just then the moon was darkened by a cloud and I flopped down, very exhausted, beside a minute bush of camel thorn. The pack passed by and I could see and hear them searching around. When I got up I was again seen and chased, but they again lost sight of me when I repeated the previous imitation of a bit of scrub. Leaving a standing patrol near the wadi, they eventually went back to camp. I heard one of them say, "They are probably only food thieves". After making a detour I came back to the deep wadi higher up. In the bright moonlight I could see the wadi winding inland. Everything was very still. I waited there for some time for Welsh, calling him softly. There was no sign of him, so I walked on towards the R/V.

Here, to my joy, the jeep, with Sergeant Ollerenshaw and Blaney, the next relief, and Corporal Leach were waiting. They had heard and seen the shooting and Very lights in our direction, but in any case they did not intend to go to the road without seeing me, for the great news had come. "S" Patrol had established a new road-watch west of Sirte yesterday. Our watch was at an end. Cantley, too, with his Patrol, had arrived the previous day, and as proof of this I was handed that supreme panacea, a cigarette.

This story is already too long to enter into the details of Welsh's adventures that night. Briefly, he evaded the first German pursuers, waited for me for an hour, became involved in three more enemy camps and was shot at in two of them, displaying much courage and ingenuity in escaping. He reached the R/V just before dawn, shortly after I had left with the jeep party for our camp. I wanted to warn the others to move to the Indian Patrol's camp, some miles to the south of ours, as the enemy might have found Welsh and would then chase us further. We therefore drove back to camp just before dawn, reaching it at first light. Here I found that the Indian Patrol had taken Bernard Bruce away to their camp further south and I ordered my Patrol to proceed there, while I returned in the jeep alone to look for Welsh.

161

I missed his footsteps on the outward journey to the R/V, but I picked them up there and tracked him until I found him near our camp-site, having walked twenty miles from the R/V. We were both glad to see each other. From his footsteps I knew, two hours before, that he was alive. He thought the Germans had hit me when he last saw me fall in the wadi. He had been much concerned in trying to remember details of the previous day's traffic, since I had the notebook. He climbed into the jeep beside me and we drove to the camp of Indian No.1 Patrol. Next morning we started on our homeward journey to Kufra, accompanied by Cantley and his Patrol. On our way we were informed that the Zella oasis had been evacuated by the enemy and we were to proceed there at once. Headquarters were moving up there too. It was only 150 miles south-west.

Our journey to Zella was slow but peaceful, with a long sleep at night. On 15 December we could hear the guns of the New Zealand Division making its flank attack in the very area where our road-watch had just ceased. Our Fords limped home, continually requiring major surgical operations by Indian No.1 Patrol's fitter, and were finally taken on tow. The gallant jeep nearly met its end on an Italian box mine.

As soon as we reached the track running into Zella from Hofra one could see plenty of recent tyre marks. I was, as usual, driving the jeep. Blaney, next to me with his twin Vickers "K", looked a bit anxious. I peered ahead at the tyre marks looking for an interruption or irregularity. I kept going at about 6 mph. The track came to a bend where there were a number of black rocks on either side. When I stopped we were not more than 1ft from where the tyre pattern looked odd. That was where the enemy had hidden their first of several box mines laid on the track. We found other box mines laid off the track which were easy to find from the footmarks in the sand. I uncovered and detonated them.

Bernard Bruce was quickly recovering and was restored to good health by the time we reached Zella on 20 December. Jake Easonsmith had arrived with an advance party of Group Headquarters and some of the other Patrols, including G.2 and Anthony Kinsman. Ken Sweeting, who had been commanding G.2 Patrol, had been evacuated to Cairo.

Zella is an Arab village of considerable importance and antiquity with archways over some streets and around the main square. There were plenty of good wells and date palms, donkeys and goats. It was just the sort of oasis I had hankered after in my travels in North Africa six and a half years earlier, during my summer vacation from Cambridge (I had driven alone from London to Cairo, 11,000 miles, nearly half of it in Morocco). A really beautiful small kid goat, on a bit of cord, dirty compared with the kid's immaculate whiteness, was brought to me by the Mudir of Zella. He arrived at the head of a small delegation. His white beard and white burnous gave him an air of distinction. He had assumed I was the chief of the new bandwaggon. Jake Easonsmith with his small party of Group HQ, was not selected to take part in the ceremony. With Cantley's Indian Patrol I had arrived at the head of about forty-five men.

After some attempted conversation, and gestures denoting the Mudir's welcome and his relief that the Italians had gone, he presented me with the goat kid in the proud and deferential manner of a maître-d'hotel. I was expected, of course, to eat, not to admire, it. Gastronomy, not aesthetics, was his concern. I took the bleating white creature with an air of gratitude – and admiration – which I really did feel. The delegation then left us alone with our timely gift. It was, after all, Christmas Eve. Mudir though he was, he was unlikely to be confused about giving us a paschal offering at the wrong season.

"What do I do with it?" asked Guardsman Scourey, when I handed it to him. He was acting as our cook and had some tins of Meat and Vegetables (M & V) on the boil. All my Patrol admired our new pet, but our previous ones, two cheetah cubs, had not survived long. In any case they were leaving on an operation the next day. There was no solution other than for one of us to hand the kid over to someone in the village not too near the Mudir's household. I am not squeamish. We had shot and eaten a gazelle on patrol, but nothing as delicate and defenceless as this. We all wished we had not seen or heard it.

From now on "G" Patrol was too reduced in numbers to operate in two separate Patrols. G.1 had only six Other Ranks out of the twenty that started from Kufra on 29 November. Twelve were captured on the way out. Two had been discovered by the enemy on road-watch. I learned later than none of our men had been wounded. Some of them escaped after Italy capitulated, walking 450 miles to rejoin 8th Army in Italy. Though mindful of our lost companions, the Patrol celebrated Christmas

Eve here at Zella around our camp fire. A successor to Sergeant Fraser was found who could make a fair imitation of the original rum punch, though scarcely as resourceful in its ingredients as G.1's Hogmanay brew at Jalo twelve months before. Bernard Bruce appeared to shake off the last of his recent ague in as spirited a war-dance as had ever been seen in darkest Africa. Our guest, Donny Player, 2nd in Command of the Sherwood Rangers, on the other hand, who was due to accompany Bernard on his next operation, did not presume too much on our hospitality and did not, like many of his "G" Patrol hosts, require carrying off to his sleeping bag.

At dawn on Christmas Day the Patrol moved off on its next job, to reconnoitre a route north-west, across the rugged country inland from Buerat el Hosn and Misurata where Montgomery was contemplating another left hook, this time to Tripoli. I watched it head off NW from the palm trees of Zella under its new Commander, Captain Bernard Bruce, accompanied by Major Donny Player and Lieutenant Anthony Kinsman. After one and a quarter years, my last operation for the LRDG was done.

EPILOGUE

The Author continues:

"I wonder if . . ." is often a thought when going over one's past. It applies to my thinking when I left the LRDG on Christmas Day 1942 at the Zella oasis south of Sirte. An old Bombay, once an 80 mph bomber, took off from the landing strip, full of crates of drink for the RAF, Fernback, my soldier servant who replaced Wann, and me, and flew us to the large landing ground, El Adem, south of Tobruk in Cyrenaica. There we spent a jolly Christmas night as guests of the Squadron headquarters of this unit of Transport Command – jolly and not too hearty.

There then followed a few days in Cairo with Vivian Street and Peter Oldfield, one or other of them due to take over command of the SAS as David Stirling had just been captured (for the first time). I had talks with Billy McLean, who introduced me to Basil Ringrose, who had been his boss and Mark Pilkington's during their thirteen months in Abyssinia commanding brigades of deserters from the Italian Army. The suggestion was that I should join an organization shortly to be integrated with SOE for work behind enemy lines in the Balkans and Mediterranean area. I suppose I might have gone later with Billy on his Albanian party. I said, "No". I had decided to rejoin my regiment, the 2nd Battalion Scots Guards, now at a hutted camp outside Damascus, alongside the 3rd Coldstream, old comrades, and the 6th Grenadiers, who had arrived from England recently, to complete a three-battalion strong 201st Guards Brigade.

To rejoin one's battalion is rather like going home again. One has many old friends. When detached, as I had been for nearly a year and a half, one felt anxious about them and hoped that they were doing well and not being mauled too much. The Battle of Gazala had seen the over-running of most of the Scots Guards by the Germans on Rigel Ridge a few months earlier. Their 6-pounders had been delivered just as the battle was beginning, with no time to train on these replacements for the 2-pounders. The 6-pounder, properly handled and sited (sometimes difficult in the desert), could more than hold its own against the German Mark III and IV tanks, as we later proved at Medenine.

I also felt I had been lucky to have been offered the job of Scots Guards officer with the LRDG and I owed them a debt for giving me such a chance. Another reason for my going back to the regiment was that I think that change, up to a point well short of revolution, is a good thing. Robin Gurdon and I had often discussed this during the three months or so when we were at Siwa. We both felt that one can get stale, so as to justify a policy of letting someone else have a go. Roughly speaking, we felt that a guardsman might go back to his battalion after six months unless there were special reasons for keeping him, such as being a trained navigator. In Robin Gurdon's case there had been a strong possibility of David Stirling offering him the job of 2nd-in-Command. Ever since Jock Lewes was killed in January 1942 the SAS had suffered from a lack of detail in administration and David was well aware of this. The offer was never officially made, as Robin was killed in July. He would have been just the man for the job.

I think Robin would have accepted David's offer in spite of their differences in attitude towards the war. He may even have actually done so without my knowing. Robin wanted to win the war just as much as David did, but a good deal more methodically. He admired David's dash, imagination and persuasiveness, as we all did. It would have been an advantage being about twelve years older.

Our Commanding Officer, Guy Prendergast, was a devolutionist: leave responsibility to those who are in a position to exercise it wisely. If, as a Patrol commander, you wanted your men to shave back at base, or wear a distinctive bit of clothing or paint your trucks pink, you were usually free to do so. You also had complete discretion in tactical matters, such as how to accomplish an operation. So when I and our supporting regiments, the officers commanding the battalions of Coldstream and Scots Guards, wanted to make changes in personnel, Colonel Guy would willingly fall in with our wishes.

After a long spell away, I think I did the right thing in rejoining my battalion outside Damascus. It was ironical that I should travel nearly two thousand miles east and north and then to have to go in the reverse direction for almost the same distance. Within two months of arriving in Syria I was at Medenine in Tunisia, only four hundred and fifty miles north-west of Zella.

My company commander, Ray Lewthwaite, was wounded in the early part of the German tank attack on us at Medenine (or Tadjera Khir) when I took over command until I was carted back to Tripoli in an ambulance for two and a half days from a night attack north of Enfidaville, near the end of the Tunisian campaign. I had been wounded on 25 April 1943 by an Italian hand grenade.

Prendergast kindly wrote to me just before we reached Enfidaville, where the mountain ridges, running west-east, are a real menace, asking me to rejoin the LRDG as a squadron commander (there were only two) when they were preparing for the disastrous attempt to take Cos and Leros and the Aegean islands. But there was no choice for me then. I was happy and lucky to be in command of "G" Company Scots Guards for as long as possible.

I could have accepted a job as "Wing Commander" at the Middle East Staff College at Haifa after I recovered from my wound and rejoined my Battalion near Tunis, but I didn't. I went on to land at Salerno, still as a Company Commander, from Tripoli on 9 September 1943. Italy was a brutal and beautiful country to fight in. After two months we had thirty-seven officer casualties in our battalion, which had landed with twenty-five. Of these, sixteen were killed. I was lucky to last as far as the first Monte Camino battle, but that was the end of active warfare for me; six weeks in hospital in Naples, seven weeks near Algiers and then hospitals in England for a long time. My first remission from nursing for a short spell in April 1945, and long one in 1946, gave me the opportunity to write this story about my time with the Long Range Desert Group.

Ian Weston-Smith writes:

Alastair Timpson had a warm welcome, which combined affection with admiration, when he rejoined 2nd Battalion

Scots Guards during its re-formation in Syria in January 1943.

We had all been proud of "G" Patrol LRDG, especially as Michael Crichton Stuart and Alastair had successively commanded it. I have no doubt the Coldstream felt the same way about their contribution to the Patrol. Timpson, as he was often called in a way which somehow summed up with a touch of humour his unusual qualities, had the genuine pioneer spirit, a determination to venture physically and mentally, quite often regardless of, or even sometimes cocking a snook at, authority.

There was a certain seriousness in his attitude which he would banish with a sharp but kindly sense of humour from which, once it had found one's weak spot, the irony was gently withdrawn. He had a basic love of adventure imbued, perhaps, in his American blood, and it took many forms – the famous Cambridge to Cambridge via London walk in 24 hours; a very close inspection of Austria just after the Anschluss; introducing Cazenove-style stockbroking to Beirut; inspecting (in the deepest sense) gold mines in South Africa, and, of course, the LRDG. In the summer of 1941 Alastair had joined us in "Left Flank" Company at Buq Buq after the June battle which had failed to relieve Tobruk. He got a warm welcome and our spirits rose when after a ritual couple of glasses of Duggan's Dew (as whisky was then known) he announced that he had brought a case of champagne. Ronald Orr-Ewing was not amused: "Young officers do NOT arrive with cases of champagne," he pronounced. The temperature fell. It was all of 24 hours before Ronald said, "Now, what's happened to that bubbly, Timpson?"

I was wounded at Agedabia in December 1941 and our paths did not cross again until Tunisia. We subsequently met in the Salerno beachhead. It was a timely encounter at Julian Gascoigne's Brigade HQ in the early morning of 11 September 1943 and Alastair was eating a hearty breakfast from the back of a P/U. I joined him. My job was liaison between Lou Lyne, who was commanding the Queen's Brigade, and Brigadier Julian who was commanding the Guards Brigade. Lyne had sent me over to say that the German mortars were formidable and that there were snipers close to Gascoigne's HQ. This news was received with scorn. Moments later a Mark IV tank opened up on us and we dived for the ditch. I felt quite pleased.

Alastair had been sent to report on the daylight attack of the previous day on the "Tobacco" factory, which had met with some success and then gone badly wrong when the Germans had reinforced with tanks and mortars.

We knew of course that on the previous day a mortar bomb on the crossroads had killed Hal Astley Corbett and wounded Michael Crichton Stuart and Sweetie Romer, so it was a surprise to find Colonel Guy Taylor (who commanded the Scots Guards) on the same crossroads, and even more unexpected was the appearance of the Divisional Commander and a short visit from the Corps Commander. I was half-expecting Alex! Things were not going according to plan. The Salerno landing, which launched the Allied campaign to drive the German forces from Italy, presented Hitler and Kesselring with a dilemma – to yield ground and thus airfields, slowly and expensively for the Allies, or to withdraw and concentrate defensive strategy on Russia and the Western Front. Hitler decided not to withdraw, so Rome was to be held at all costs and that of course meant that Cassino and the Gustav and Hitler Lines would be obstacles of determined ferocity.

After the Generals left the order group, Colonel Guy Taylor told me I had been released by Lou Lyne and was to command "F" Company in the forthcoming night attack. Tony Philipson, who was temporarily in command after Michael was wounded, looked glum, but he didn't glower and as we were old friends I felt comfortable. "Let's go and do a recce," said Alastair and I felt relieved. He had taken "G" Company right into the "Tobacco" Factory in the previous day's daylight attack, and only had to withdraw because he had no anti-tank guns to hold the German counter-attack. It was a thorough reconnaissance which told us a lot about the lie of land, from Ralph Dolland's O/P on the railway, and from the top floor of the farmhouse where the gunners had their O/P. But we gleaned nothing as to the strength of the garrison, and I can still see the look of doubt on Alastair's face as we parted. Once or twice we discussed the likelihood of the "Tobacco" Factory (it was in fact a cannery) being reinforced. Certainly one "88" had been active, as a Scots Greys tank had almost learnt the hard way. But doubts are one thing, suggesting to one's battalion commander that he should think again about a night attack, so urgently required by the Top Brass, is quite another. I made my attack with the three platoons of "F" Company in brilliant moonlight. It was a fairly desperate business because two of the platoon commanders (William

Beckett and Roddy McLeod) were killed, and only Tony Philipson, Corporal Archibald and myself got anywhere near the objective, which was the buildings in front of the crucial crossroads on the German line of communication. We plunged into the midst of three Spandau crews; after waiting three hours for the moon to wane they came to find us and we were captured.

Of Alastair and "G" Company on our right we knew nothing. He had in fact got right into the Factory and could have stayed there if he had had anti-tank support. On his right Archie Elliott and Ian Fraser were prisoners, with many of their platoons, after a tough battle. The enemy were 16th Panzer Division, fully re-equipped after Stalingrad, and there was just a faint and feeble consolation in knowing that our enemy had such a track record. It was two years before Alastair and I could compare notes and I can remember him saying that when he got Colonel Guy Taylor on the radio he had virtually insisted on withdrawal, the alternative being large casualties and many prisoners. This was, I remember thinking, typical of his independence and self-reliance – a whiff of the frontiersman, treating authority with the measured disrespect it sometimes deserves. He was, above all, a fighting soldier: he could be quite bloody-minded, but nobody thought any the less of him for it.

The Editor concludes:

After a determined German attack was beaten off by the Coldstream and Scots Guards, and the position in the beach-head elsewhere stabilized, the Salerno battle swung in the Allies' favour. They were able to advance out of the beachhead towards Naples, the Germans eventually withdrawing into the formidable Winter Line, between that city and Rome.

A bastion of the Winter Line was Monte Camino, a rocky 3000-foot feature. The Coldstream attacked Calabritto village and a lower spur of the mountain; from there the Grenadiers and Scots Guards assaulted up Barearse Ridge; together they clung to advanced positions under heavy counter-attacks and shelling. On the third night, 11–12 November 1943, Alastair's company headquarters was hit by a shell: several men were killed and others, including the company second-in-command,

Nigel Barne, injured, and Alastair himself was severely wounded. Barne remembers that Alastair was insistent on receiving first-aid attention after everyone else. With great difficulty he was, like the others, evacuated by stretcher. He said goodbye to Company Sergeant Major Little who had been with him since Tunisia. (Next day Little was killed by spandau fire.) Alastair was carried by eight men down the mountain's slippery and shell-swept tracks. He was not to fight again.

And so the story of courage, endurance and determination, of duty conscientiously carried out in circumstances frequently of great physical hardship and of ever-present danger, is done. As I have progressed in my work on this book, I have found my admiration for the author steadily increasing. He seems to have excelled both as a leader of irregular forces and as a regimental officer.

In my Preface I remarked on the fact that Alastair Timpson's memoir is written in an unemotional way, apparently strictly as a military record and (with certain exceptions) without going into much detail about his relations with the men under his command. The fly-leaf to this book contains a quotation from T.E.Lawrence's famous work *Seven Pillars of Wisdom* and it is tempting to compare the two men. In fact there is no comparison, except that both did great things for their country in a desert environment. Apart from the fact that Timpson was commanding his own countrymen, while Lawrence led and inspired men of another race, they were entirely different sorts of men, and they told their stories in entirely different ways. In Lawrence's matchless prose the emotional and dramatic content was always high. Not so in Timpson's restrained and reserved style. To illustrate this, one may consider the story of his last epic operation, told in Chapter Nine, for which he was to receive his Military Cross. After he and Guardsman Welsh had completed a long and arduous road-watch, they were detected, fired on and chased. Separated, they both had hair-raising and exhausting experiences. Both walked more than twenty miles across the burning desert before Timpson, now jeep-borne, finally found Welsh. Timpson simply says, "We were both glad to see each other". Well, yes.

But there was indeed a human being inside the soldier, and I conclude with an extract from Alastair Timpson's obituary notice in the Scots Guards Regimental Magazine, written by Captain the Marquess of Aberdeen, a former brother-officer:

"On demobilization he went into stockbroking with Cazenove. He went to Beirut in a determined and original attempt to get the Arabs interested. But the Suez crisis intervened, making the British *persona non grata*.

"Those of you who never knew him may get the impression when reading about his military career that he was an austere figure. Nothing of the sort – he loved people, men and women alike. As a present serving officer said, 'He was such fun'. Like so many of us he enjoyed going over shared war experiences, invariably remembering the odd and the hilarious. Our women would say that we never grew up, but Alastair was excused by the women because he knew how to enchant them and not bother them with male reminiscence.

"He sparked with a zest for life and when he came to be dying he was brave and stoical. We shall miss him and all our sympathy goes to his wife and family."

I think that is quite a good note on which to end this book.

EDITOR'S BIBLIOGRAPHICAL NOTE

A serious bibliography is not to be expected in a work of this nature. However, in the original version of his memoir the author did refer in the text and in footnotes to some books, and it is thought that the following may be helpful.

The general story of the war in the Western Desert has been told in innumerable books. An especially good account is given in *The Battle for North Africa – 1940–1943* by W.G.F.Jackson (Mason/Charter, New York 1975) which itself contains a full bibliography, as well as references to all the relevant official sources. General Sir William Jackson commanded a Field Squadron, Royal Engineers, in 6th Armoured Division in Tunisia.

Many readers will be familiar with the well-known biographies of Erwin Rommel by Brigadier Peter Young and (more recently) General Sir David Fraser, and with the various biographies of Montgomery. There are also many accounts of the El Alamein Battle. The best one I know is *Alamein* by C.E.Lucas Phillips (Heinemann, London 1962). The author, a Gunner officer, was present at the battle and he covers it very well.

Good accounts of the Long Range Desert Group are given in David Lloyd Owen's *The Desert my Dwelling Place* (Cassell, 1957) and *Providence Their Guide* (Harrap, 1980). The author is mentioned several times by Alastair Timpson as a Patrol Commander. On 4 October 1997 he unveiled the Memorial to the Long Range Desert Group at a Service of Dedication in the Guards Chapel. Also worth consulting is W.B.Kennedy-Shaw's *Long Range Desert Group* (Collins, 1945).

The Guards Patrol, from its inception in winter 1940 up to Alastair Timpson's joining it in September 1941, is covered in *G Patrol*, by his Scots Guards predecessor Michael Crichton Stuart (William Kimber, London 1958).

There have also been a number of books wholly or partly about the Special Air Service in its early days, notably Virginia Cowles' biography of David Stirling *The Phantom Major* (Collins, London 1958).

I also mention two other enjoyable books by veterans of the early SAS: *The Drums of Memory* (Leo Cooper, London 1996) by a former 2nd Scots Guards officer Sir Stephen Hastings, and *When the Grass Stops Growing* (Leo Cooper, London 1997) by Sir Carol Mather. He and Jock Lewes, the first SAS second-in-command, were the only two Welsh Guards officers to serve in the Western Desert. Both these autobiographical works give a vivid picture of the conditions of life in the desert, and of the daring operations in which the LRDG were so closely involved.

There were other irregular units in the desert, and some account of them (besides good coverage of the LRDG and SAS) is given in Julian Thompson's *"War Behind Enemy Lines"* (Sidgwick & Jackson, London 1998). Prominent was Popski's Private Army, the story of which was written by its commander, Major Vladimir Peniakoff, in *Private Army* (Jonathan Cape, London 1950). This very individual unit survived the end of the Desert War and did good work in the High Apennines of Italy. At the war's end they got themselves over the Alps into Austria, where they were quartered next door to the 3rd Battalion Welsh Guards in which I was serving. I remember that they had some nice Polish girls with them, and that every night from their mess came the agreeable sounds of music, laughter and breaking glass. Very soon they were disbanded.

To my knowledge, there has never been a proper history of 22nd, then 200th, finally 201st Guards Brigade, although for those who have access to such material it is possible to piece the story together from the regimental histories. There is however one recent book, *Esprit de Corps* by W.A.Elliott (Michael Russell, Norwich 1966), which recounts the later story of 2nd Battalion Scots Guards from the time he joined them in Tripoli before the Salerno landing. The book tells us much about the attitude and methods of those old desert hands.

Some of the same ground (viz. the fighting at Salerno) is also covered in *The High Road Back to England* (Michael Russell, Norwich, 1999) by Sir Ian Fraser.

Finally, those who wish to pursue the story of the pre-war explorers should read *Libyan Sands: Travel in a Dead World* by R.A.Bagnold (Hodder & Stroughton, London 1935) and *Desert Explorer* by Peter Clayton (Zerzura Press, Two Rivers, Car Green, Saltash, Cornwall, 1997). The author of the latter book is the son of Pat Clayton who was a pre-war explorer colleague of Lieutenant-Colonel Ralph Bagnold, and commanded the famous long-range expedition to Fezzan and Chad in winter 1940–41. The pre-war explorers never found the lost oasis of Zerzura, or any trace of King Cambyses' vanished army; but they made possible the development of a unique body of fighting men, the fame of whose exploits shines over the years.

INDEX

179

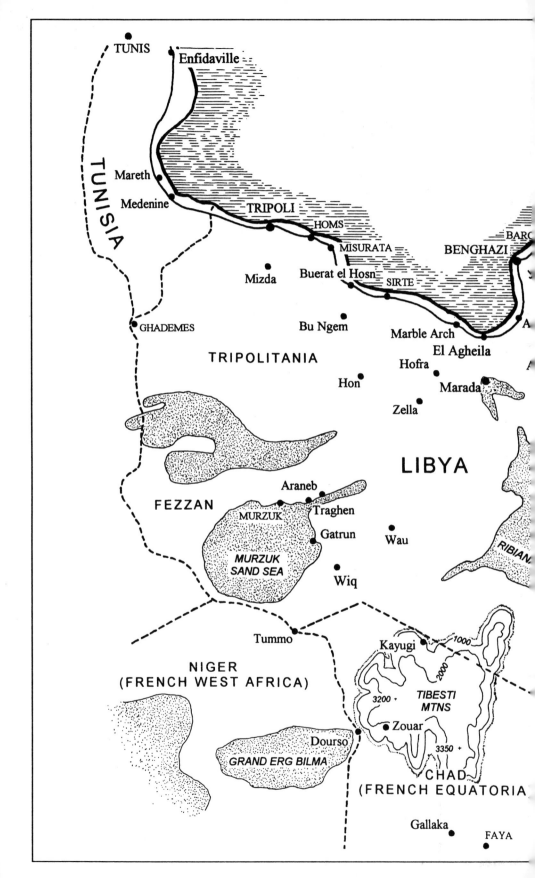